Business Improve
for Professionals

by Nick Jones

A book in two sections:-

1. **Think Twice, Cut Once** - The Business Cube and Understanding your Business.

2. **The Russian Dolls** - Implementing Business Improvements.

First published in the United Kingdom in 2022 by NBJ Business Solutions Ltd.

ISBN 978-1-9161205-0-1

Produced by The Choir Press

Contents

Section 1: Think Twice, Cut Once

Section 2: The Russian Dolls

Preface

Ever wondered why so many business improvements fail?

The evidence is littering the commercial landscape. And many failures are spectacular: the business either implodes (Carillion plc., officially the largest ever trading liquidation in the UK), or explodes (TSB, Trustee Savings Bank plc.) and reveals that last year's massive IT failure cost the bank £330m, with 80,000 customers switching their account to a competitor.

And there are hundreds of·books and media events that explore the demise of one BI after another. Many are best-sellers, with excellent analyses of what went wrong, who is responsible, and why it happened. It's like a business autopsy, with failure laid out for all to see.

Well, we have a few autopsies in both Sections of this book: but this book is not about BI autopsies. It's about what you have to do to avoid BI failure. And this book is quite clear about the steps involved in achieving this, based on one fundamental fact: the majority of BIs undertaken fail. Estimates vary as to the exact number: experts disagree over the percentage of failures: but not one that I've read has disputed the fact that the majority fail. Why? Take a typical list from a small IT consulting company written in Forbes magazine in February 2020.

1. Not digging to the root causes of the problem.
2. Not involving the right people.
3. Not building a problem-solving culture.

The reasons seem plausible: they align with explanations from many other authors: yet how do you deliver these requirements? As Einstein has said, 'We cannot solve our problems with the same thinking we used when we created them'. And if that is true, then something new and different is required.

This book focuses on a different approach to **understanding** any Business Improvement **before starting** the **Implementation.** So there's the **Business Cube** to structure and discipline the thinking around BIs. Then there's an **Implementation Model** that channels this understanding into a structured approach to effectively delivering the BIs. Using a blend of Russian Dolls, the Logical Levels Model from neuro-linguistic programming, and data/information relevant to the BI, then you will radically improve the odds that your BI will be successful.

Because most BIs are flawed from the very beginning: they are built to fail, from inception, and the hard work you're doing at the front-end of the BI is creating the seeds of its future failure. I'll quote the Head of the Infrastructure and Projects Authority in the UK: 'that we really have construction projects in infrastructure that look the same today as they did 40 years ago. There is a huge opportunity to use modern methods of construction and tools that will bring significant improvements in productivity. I am not talking about marginal percentages, but 30%, 40% improvement.' (Transport Committee Oral evidence: Major transport infrastructure projects: appraisal and delivery, HC 24, 12th May 2021). I'll take the HS2 rail improvement project as being a business improvement. So there's room for improved performance here! And to summarize what the reader will be covering.....

In a Nutshell

1. Before starting any business improvements, you need to <u>understand</u> your whole business.
2. That understanding is in terms of the Resources, Standards and Management Systems.
3. **Resources** are the 'People', 'Parts and Process', 'Products and Services'.
4. **Standards** embrace 'Quality/Safety', 'Quantity' and 'Time'.
5. **Management Systems** involve 'Forecast/Plan', 'Control', and 'Report/Review'.

Understanding before Implementing

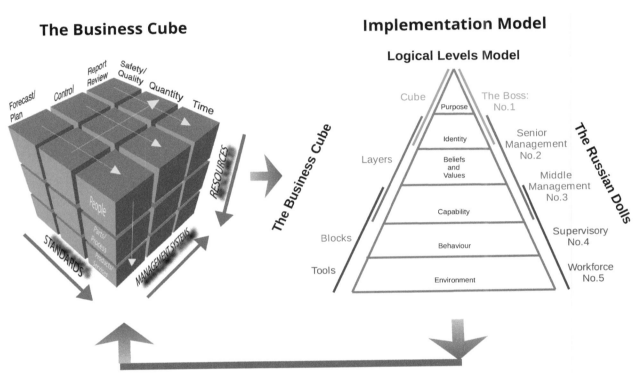

Business Improvement Results

6. When you have understood your whole business, then start thinking about BIs.
7. Take the understanding you've gained from the **The Business Cube**, and transfer across to the **Implementation Model** - align data/information according to the appropriate Level - i.e. The Boss and Senior Management <u>need to understand</u> the whole business.
8. Using the the principles of the Logical Levels Model, align the Business Improvement changes with the appropriate **Russian Doll** - so Supervisors focus on Beliefs and Values, Capability, Behaviour and the Environment. There's a certain overlap, which is shown in the **Implementation Model**, yet it's clear where the boundaries are.
9. Track the Business Improvement Results as they flow through your business. Repeat the methodology whenever you want or need to, remembering the twenty seven Blocks inside The Business Cube, and the five Russian Dolls who will lead and manage the BIs. And that's it in one side of A4 paper.

.... The Complete Business Improvement Model

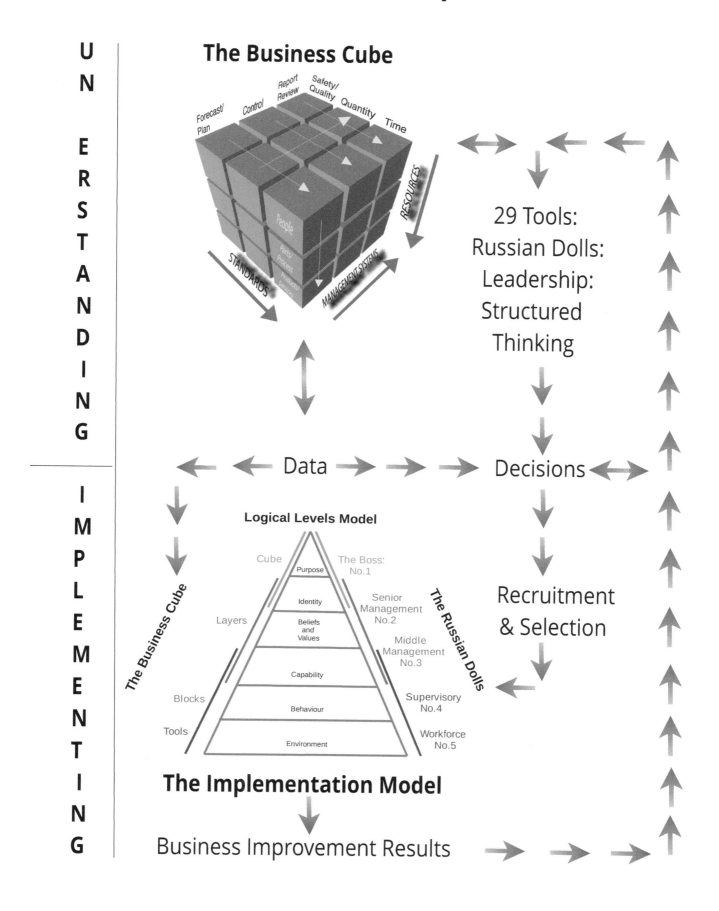

Using this Book

It's designed for readers who want to 'dip' into the text at any point, pull out ideas that interest them, and then understand if those ideas are relevant for their current business needs. The business improvement opportunities will often be prompted by a need - whether that need is a gentle nudge or a fire alarm sounding, depends on the boss's level of attention to their responsibilities and awareness of the business environment.

And it's in two sections - for those readers who are more interested in understanding their business, or are more concerned with implementing the improvements that they've already decided upon. Or you can buy both sections, and follow the BI story all the way through. Whichever way you choose, 'Business Improvements for Professionals' is dedicated to those of you who just want to understand their business and get on with improving it.

So enjoy reading and keep driving those initiatives.

Any comments or criticisms, additions or omissions, please contact the author:-

nickcbjones59@gmail.com
(44) 7933 024439
nbj@businesssolutions.com

The content is entirely the responsibility of the author: any flaws in spelling and grammar are likewise. If you, or your business, are interested in developing Business Improvements for yourselves, please feel free to contact me. Have fun!

---

1. Think Twice, Cut Once[1]

by Nick Jones

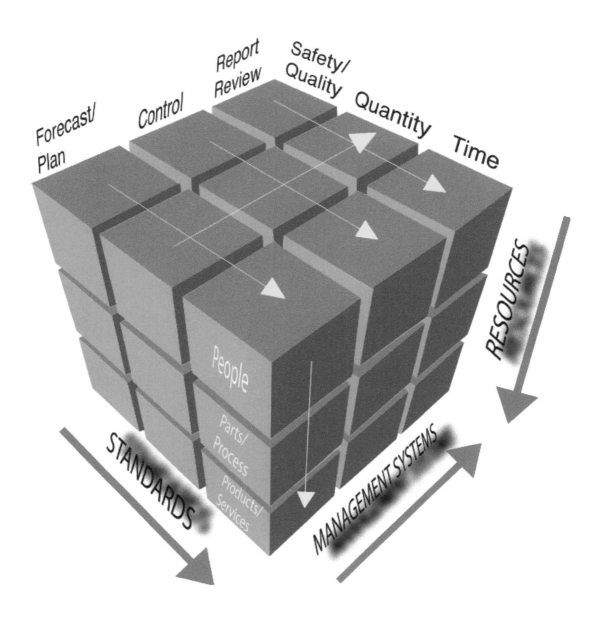

Preface

Sitting in a cramped office in a large manufacturing company located in Argentina, we compared the prices of our new digital watches. The gentleman seated opposite won: his watch was cheaper than mine. Then he said, 'I need to take US$1m. out of this operation in the next seven days'. And that's where my story begins.

To permanently remove US$1m. from the cost-base of a medium-sized loss-making company in a week is difficult: to do it when you've only just arrived on-site is even more challenging. We approached the cost reduction by aligning product demand with hours required to manufacture at that level of demand: then looking at the indirect costs that were available without impacting the production capacity: then matching these numbers with their latest organization chart. We achieved his business goal with a few hours to spare before the deadline: the new owner was delighted, and the business improvement (BI) moved forward.

What did I learn from all of this? Firstly, a business improvement initiative of this scope and speed of execution can only be delivered with the full support of the Boss. That is the person at the top of the business who has made the decision to start the project. And secondly, there had to be a better way of organizing the information, crunching the numbers, and delivering a set of agreed actions that could be implemented immediately. So BI success is dependent on the **support and drive of the Boss** and a comprehensive **structure** that encompasses the BI within the whole business.

This book examines the role of the Boss in business improvements, and then explains the use of the **Business Cube** methodology. There is plenty of literature on the first item, and very little on the second, mainly because the Cube is a new methodology for understanding and improving the performance of any business.

So you can read the entire book if you want to, or just the overview if you're busy. Either way, have fun, enjoy the book, and then dramatically increase the success rate of your business improvements.

Contents

Overview

This book offers a structured approach to improving the ***profitability***[4] of your business. To achieve this, we use the ***Business Cube***, which combines the key components of any business: ***resources, standards*** and ***management systems***. Breaking these three components into their parts, you have the following:-

Resources[5] -   ***People, Parts*** and ***Process, Products*** and ***Services.***
Standards[6] -   ***Quality*** and ***safety, Quantity*** and ***Time.***
Management Systems[7] -   ***Forecast*** and ***Plan, Control, Report*** and ***Review***

And this is represented by the ***'Business Cube'*** format.

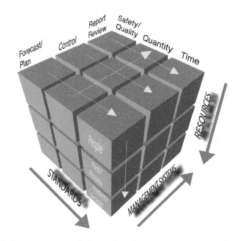

Inside the Cube, there are 3 Layers and 27 Blocks. For example, Block 1 combines the 'People', 'Forecast and Plan', 'Safety and Quality' elements - what I prefer to think of as 'a cube of three equal terms.' By definition, just re-structuring a business in this way **requires you to think of a business** in these terms. So if we continue with the example of Block 1, then the contents could be:-

Headcount, full-time equivalents (FTEs), people allowances, master schedule, recruitment & selection, training needs analysis, training gaps, skill sets, future skill requirements, redeployment, business alignment, safety policy & compliance, safety assessment, safety dashboard, quality policy & compliance, quality design skills, bench-marking, activity-based costing, people development, mentoring, flexibility, leadership, future technical advances, Government policy, legislation, trade and deal compliance, grants and concessions.

This provides an actual framework for structured thinking - and it's this framework that we call the 'Business Cube'. The Cube comes with clear rules for use, that are applicable for all businesses: and they capture everything about any business. No more 'thinking outside of the box'!: more about thinking inside the Cube.

We'll show you how to think about the hierarchy that is actually running the business - and why it is critically important that the Boss owns the Business Improvements. A different approach to the traditional organization chart or matrix: an approach more aligned to delivering the improvements, rather than some 'work-around' approaches that try to get your improvements to fit everybody's expectations. And this is where the Dolls come into play - and 'Doll & Cubes' can be such a powerful tool to reinvigorate the business. Begin with Step 1 (Doll No.1: Boss), you can follow this simple flow:-

The Business Cube Process Flow

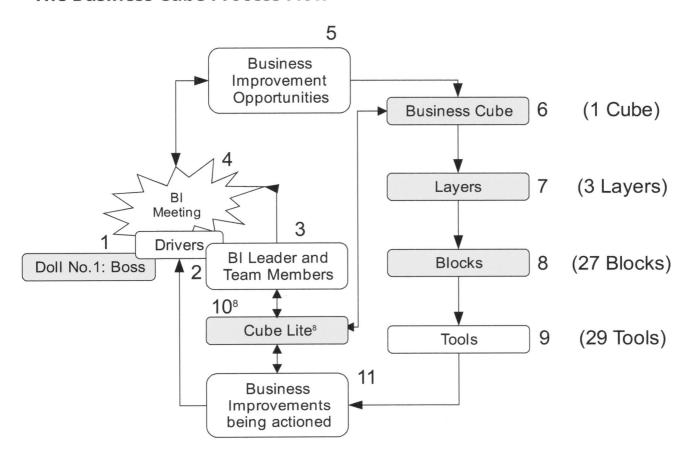

Starting with **[1]**, *Doll No. 1: Boss*, this is the person who decided to initiate the Business Improvement)BI). Move to the *Drivers* **[2]**: these are the reasons the Boss started the BI. There needs to be a detailed description of exact scope of the initiative. **[3]** Be clear about who the Team Leader and Team Members are. The BI Meeting **[4]** is when the sponsor, the BI group and other invited people agree the Initiative. So far, the first four Steps are consensus-building, and **[5]** are the Improvements they are planning. **And this is where the Business Cube [6] kicks in**. It takes the thinking and discussions of the group and structures it into a comprehensive format. The Layers **[7]**, Blocks **[8]** and Tools **[9]** take that output and focus the effort on achieving the BI **[11]**. Reference to the **Business Cube [6]** is done through **Cube Lite**[8] **[10]**, which just allows the project Team to remind themselves of all the issues and items that came out of the original Business Cube meeting. Here, the Business Opportunity is realised with a measurable reduction in the amount of time and effort to achieve the agreed Business Improvements. Basically, the group can achieve more benefits with less effort by cutting resource time spent and rework incurred. Which means that the group can review with **[1]** *the Boss,* knowing they have optimized their investment in BI.

The Boss's role in this process flow is critical for a successful outcome: the role of the 'Business Cube' is to provide a tangible structure on which to position [or 'hang'] your 'Structured Thinking': and the two together offer a far greater chance of delivering business improvements, on-time, within budget and to the required standard of performance.

So let's get going! .....starting with those beautiful Russian Dolls.......

1. Russian Dolls - Leadership

Overwhelmed - one word that comes to mind after seven days of intensive work: and a certain knowledge that there had to be a better way of understanding a business. In any company employing 600 people, there's a mountain of information, some fact, some fiction. So the first step is to focus on the facts: and not all these are accurate. Then you can breeze through a series of studies, mostly from the era of Scientific Management, that either confirm or deny the facts you've been given. Then compile and present a reasoned and quantifiable summary that shows how the required savings can be delivered.

Once the savings were agreed, there followed a period of reflection. First thoughts concerned the enormous changes that had occurred over a few days: from the company takeover to a sudden reduction in the cost-base. And all because there was a new main shareholder who had reshaped the company's future. Just one person had moved the company forward at tremendous speed: the impact of a new Boss was phenomenal.

A picture formed in my mind: the 'Matryoshka'[9] Dolls I had first seen in the GUM[10] store in Moscow in 1972 - when the Russian Federation was called the Soviet Union. The first and largest doll was the 'Boss', the most important person in the company. If you change the Boss, you have the potential to change everything within the legal and commercial framework of the company, Forget leadership, or management: just think about **the authority to implement change.** So the starting point for any business improvement (BI) is the person at the top of the company.

The First Doll - The Boss

The Boss sets the goals, standards and tempo for the whole company, getting the most business-effective person in this position is essential, particularly if you're driving for improvements. The leadership and management styles that are displayed by the Boss cascade through the entire business, and unofficially define the behavioural norms for all people in the company. The Boss has to 'own' all business improvement programmes, which means understanding and being involved in their progress and achievements. **Lesson 1: Engage and involve the Boss at all times.**

The Second Doll - Senior Management / The Top Team

I read this in a recent article[11]: 'Change programmes fail because the top management lacks commitment. Employees look to management and leadership for vision and direction, but often find leadership's position muddled and confused. This is the single biggest factor that can make or break any change programme'. If the Top Team aren't fully engaged, then you haven't complied with Lesson 1. So **Lesson 2** is simple: **Engage and involve the Top Team at all times.** And remember that the No.1 Doll might not actually have bought the Improvement Programme, but they need to be **involved in**, not just committing to, delivering the BI.

The Third Doll - Middle Management

This Doll needs constant attention - the Top Team has to demand frequent updating on all business improvements. this has to be 'built into' the routine of the manager's daily / weekly working life. Although the message is cascading from above, this is the Doll that often wants to 'manage the message', acting as a sieve through which all communications must pass. Alastair Mant[11] sums up this contradiction in his book,'Leaders We Deserve': they try hard to get along with everybody from their Supervisors to their Boss.

The Fourth Doll - Supervisors

When it comes to 'getting the improvements done', then the Supervisory level is critical for great results. This Doll can work without being micro-managed, and lead their own Teams to deliver improvements. Sometimes Managers need to just keep their Supervisors on-track, focused on delivering the promised business improvements.

The Fifth Doll - The Workforce

You can't deliver improvements without them - whether its software development, oil & gas plants or automotive production lines. this Doll makes it or breaks it for your improvements, So don't ignore them, and learn to communicate the 'Improvement' message at every opportunity. (By communicate, I mean talk 'with' people, not 'to' them.

The Dolls

Only five Dolls, each nested within the other. The Boss can have a tremendous impact on corporate performance at every level, the results of which then flow through to the P&L. The late David Ogilvy[12] described in his book 'Ogilvy on Advertising', one of his management habits almost unique to the Ogilvy & Mather advertising company. 'When someone is made head of an office in the Ogilvy & Mather chain, I send *them* a 'Matryoshka Doll from Gorky (a Russian City). if *they* have the curiosity to open it and keep opening it until *they* come to the inside of the smallest doll, *they* find this message, 'If each of us hires people who are smaller than we are, we shall become a company of dwarves. But if each of us hire people people who are bigger than we are, we shall become a company of giants'. Aiden McCullen[13] developed this theme in a 2018 article, **'Leadership in many companies is the same'.** *The same in the way it is conducted, the same in the way it is incentivized and the same in the way it is mentally charged. Leaders are often surrounded by 'Yes' people, who do not respectfully challenge the leaders' decisions'.* He goes on to say, *'When we hire from the same business schools, recruit from the same ethnicity and train everybody in the same way, we create a tribe'.*

The new Boss at the company in Argentina already had his replacement: a person so different from himself that I struggled to understand his business logic: until I later made these notes on 'Lessons Learned' from that very busy week.

1. The Top man (this was 30 years ago when the person at the top was invariably a man) is the dominant factor in all business improvements.
2. This impacts all systems, products, suppliers - every aspect of the business.
3. Supervisors are vital to success.
4. An organization chart creates more problems than solutions.
5. Focus on the value-added activities in the business.
6. Cash is King!
7. Can begin the turnaround in less than a week.

life. Although the message is cascading from above, this is the Doll that often wants to 'manage the message', acting as a sieve through which all communications must pass. Alastair Mant[11] sums up this contradiction in his book,'Leaders We Deserve': they try hard to get along with everybody from their Supervisors to their Boss.

The Fourth Doll - Supervisors

When it comes to 'getting the improvements done', then the Supervisory level is critical for great results. This Doll can work without being micro-managed, and lead their own Teams to deliver improvements. Sometimes Managers need to just keep their Supervisors on-track, focused on delivering the promised business improvements.

The Fifth Doll - The Workforce

You can't deliver improvements without them - whether its software development, oil & gas plants or automotive production lines. this Doll makes it or breaks it for your improvements, So don't ignore them, and learn to communicate the 'Improvement' message at every opportunity. (By communicate, I mean talk 'with' people, not 'to' them.

The Dolls

Only five Dolls, each nested within the other. The Boss can have a tremendous impact on corporate performance at every level, the results of which then flow through to the P&L. The late David Ogilvy[12] described in his book 'Ogilvy on Advertising', one of his management habits almost unique to the Ogilvy & Mather advertising company. 'When someone is made head of an office in the Ogilvy & Mather chain, I send *them* a 'Matryoshka Doll from Gorky (a Russian City). if *they* have the curiosity to open it and keep opening it until *they* come to the inside of the smallest doll, *they* find this message, 'If each of us hires people who are smaller than we are, we shall become a company of dwarves. But if each of us hire people people who are bigger than we are, we shall become a company of giants'. Aiden McCullen[13] developed this theme in a 2018 article, **'Leadership in many companies is the same'.** *The same in the way it is conducted, the same in the way it is incentivized and the same in the way it is mentally charged. Leaders are often surrounded by 'Yes' people, who do not respectfully challenge the leaders' decisions'.* He goes on to say, *'When we hire from the same business schools, recruit from the same ethnicity and train everybody in the same way, we create a tribe'.*

The new Boss at the company in Argentina already had his replacement: a person so different from himself that I struggled to understand his business logic: until I later made these notes on 'Lessons Learned' from that very busy week.

1.The Top man (this was 30 years ago when the person at the top was invariably a man) is the dominant factor in all business improvements.
2. This impacts all systems, products, suppliers - every aspect of the business.
3. Supervisors are vital to success.
4. An organization chart creates more problems than solutions.
5. Focus on the value-added activities in the business.
6. Cash is King!
7. Can begin the turnaround in less than a week.

The 'Boss-in-waiting' was missing from the list. In the rush to prevent the company from going into bankruptcy, this issue never entered my mind. But the concept of the Russian Doll and the approach to business improvements was firmly embedded. **Number one: the Boss is the key driver for any improvement initiative.**

Summary

The Russian Dolls constantly remind owners / managers of the importance of the No. 1 Doll - the Boss. If you are the Boss already, you may be thinking ahead to your successor, but never forget that your current position gives you the **authority to implement improvements.**

From the Boss comes the direction and pace of improvements that are required, or necessary, to **align** the whole company with the strategy that's been decided. Then the strategy gains traction and the business momentum to succeed. All the remaining four Dolls have to be aligned with the Boss so there's **clarity and focus** for the entire workforce.

An example of the No.1 Doll in business life was the late Arnold Weinstock[14] and the General Electric Company (GEC). As Alex Brummer[15] commented, '*There was nothing dreaded more for a GEC employee than the managing director reaching them at home, late in the evening, after he had been scouring the accounts. The thoroughness of his management, the tight control on costs down to the smallest washer, enabled GEC to prosper and grow in the face of the ups and downs of the UK economy in the 1970s and 1980s, when so much of British manufacturing vanished into overseas hands,.* GEC was a world class manufacturing company: so what went wrong? In a nutshell, '*his son Simon, the commercial director of GEC, contracted cancer in 1996, and died before his father had settled the succession at the company. The City insisted that Weinstock Sr. move on and, in the same year, he became emeritus chairman. Within 6 years, GEC had unravelled as an electrical conglomerate: it's value had declined from £35bn. to less than £150m'.*

In this example, the Boss's influence is very apparent: and that has not altered over the decades. Jeff Bezos, the founder and current CEO of Amazon.com Inc., exercises the same level of interventionist control within his business, and might have the same problem of 'succession' planning that bedevilled GEC. The No.1 Russian Doll is a critical factor for successful Business Improvements: but the fundamental flaw is that No.1 Dolls believe that their influence will continue long after their departure from their company: and, think assured, they do believe that it is their company. You need that level of personal ownership for any Business Improvement to be successful. So you need a clear and resilient structure to **sustain** the Improvements, and that requires a little more thought and substance than a set of five nested Dolls.

The Russian Doll message: firstly, any successful Business Improvement requires unwavering support and involvement from the Boss. Secondly, there is a need to **think through** all the factors that impact, and are impacted by, the Improvement, using the **Business Cube** to achieve this. So there needs to be a seamless fit when delivering the Improvement, and that encourages **sustainability** after the BI Leader and Team have moved on with their lives and careers.

Now it's time to introduce the Business Cube in more detail.

2. Business Cube - System and Process

'Necessity is the mother of invention' is an English language proverb. It means, roughly, that the primary driving force behind many new inventions is a 'need', a real or perceived requirement to improve all or a part of a business. My need was to create an effective Business Model to 'manage' the scale and complexities of different BI assignments, a few of which kicked off like this:-

True Story: Here's a phone conversation about how to get a Business Improvement started:-

Caller: They want you to go back to xxxxx.
NJ: But they kicked me out.
Caller: Well they found the savings.
NJ: What do you mean?
Caller: You need to get up there for Monday morning.

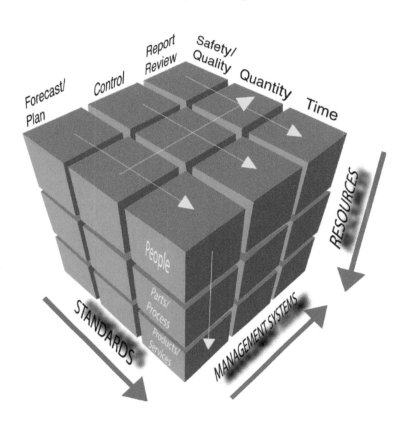

Not all business improvements are this well conceived! In this case, there was a certain vague understanding that something was seriously amiss with a large customer service centre. And the above conversation is not atypical: but it is typical of a Boss who just wants a business problem to go away. For this to happen, it requires **a structured and disciplined framework.** It is not possible to prepare and present an effective business 'way forward' on the back of a scrap of paper: it has to be organized in such a way that promotes an understanding of the issues and some insight into the solutions. This is the purpose of the Business Cube - to develop a comprehensive and logical approach for delivering business improvements of any size, from the sole trader to a conglomerate.

Let's first examine the **structure**. There are three components in this Cube: **Resources, Management Systems and Standards.** Resources are the means available to a business for improving production or profit, including plant, labour, and raw material assets. Management Systems provide the controls and the ability to manage a business. People work with each other to set goals and objectives, outline the strategies and tactics, develop the plans, schedules and necessary controls to effectively manage a company. The last component are Standards, which form 'a basis for comparison; a reference against which other things can be evaluated'.

So only three components - that's all you need to cover all the factors in Business Improvements. And this becomes evident when you examine these components.

The Business Cube Block-by-Block

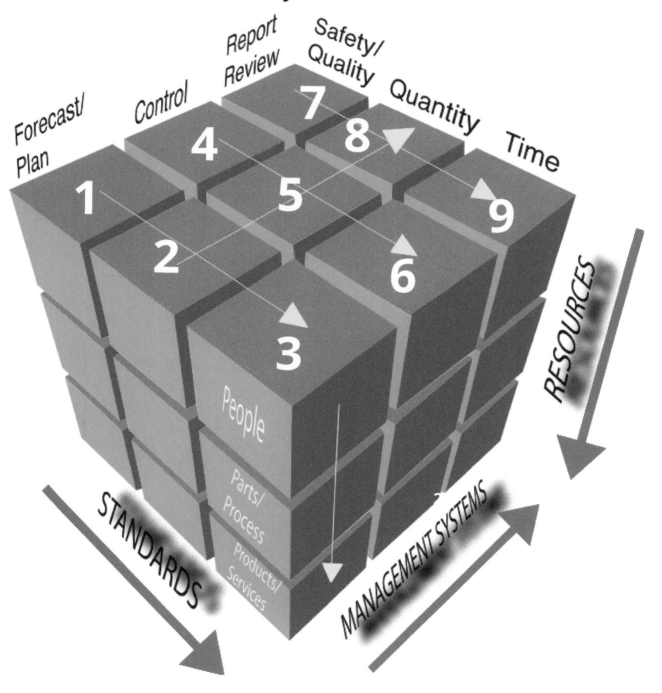

Resources	**People, Parts** and **Process, Products** and **Services**
Management Systems	**Forecast / Plan, Control, Report / Review**
Standards	**Safety / Quality, Quantity** and **Time**

So the **Structure** takes the shape of a Rubik Cube[16]. But unlike an actual Rubik, which has 26 unique miniature blocks, this Cube has 27 Blocks, That's because there's no need to rotate the Blocks: they stay in a fixed position at all times. Their structure is fixed.

And there's a **Disciplined Approach** that comes with this structure. If you study the Cube, you'll notice that there is Block 1 - or the first Block. And if there are a total of 27 Blocks in the Cube, then there have to be Blocks 2 to 27 coming after the first one. So where is the first one? Before reading the next paragraph, see if you can work it out.

Logically, there's a starting point. Let's imagine it involves 'People', and that 'Forecasting/Planning' is really important because you need to have a clear understanding of the companies future manpower requirements. The 'safety/Quality' of your people is also critical. So the Block in the upper left-hand corner fits: no other Block has those features. If you agree, then try and work out which Block is next: pause and think for a moment.

Figured it out? Move to the Block immediately below Block 1. The second Block combines 'People', 'Forecast/Plan', and 'Quantity'. People are still number one: Forecasting and Planning is essential, and this time you need to know how many people are required. Hopefully, you're beginning to understand what the Cube is asking you to do.

So the third Block is not too difficult to work out: keep moving in the same direction, towards the front of the Cube. Now the first two features in the Block remain the same, and the third one moves tp 'Time'. So if you're hiring people, you need to understand their Safety (are they fit and healthy?) and their Quality (do they have the attributes that the position demands?). Then figure out how many people you need and when you need them. So now you've checked the three Blocks that address 'People' against 'Forecast/Plan', and then against 'Safety & Quality', 'Quantity' and 'Time'.

By now you will have realized that this approach to understanding a business is different. Let's move on. The fourth Block stays with the 'People' theme within Resources, and moves to the 'Control' aspect within the Management Systems, and returning to the 'Safety & Quality' within Standards. Seems like a lot to remember: let's take some time out with a linear layout of the Cube:-

Blocks form Layers

The People

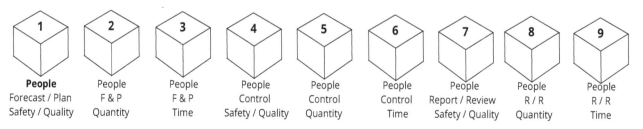

1	2	3	4	5	6	7	8	9
People	People	People	People	People	People	People	People	People
Forecast / Plan	F & P	F & P	Control	Control	Control	Report / Review	R / R	R / R
Safety / Quality	Quantity	Time	Safety / Quality	Quantity	Time	Safety / Quality	Quantity	Time

Left to right, across **the 'People' Layer** - which takes this 'Resource' and matches it against Management Systems and Standards. So then there are **9 Blocks**, each with unique parameters.   And

12

The Parts and Process Layer

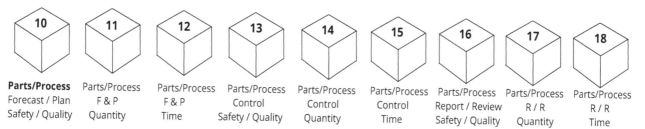

10	11	12	13	14	15	16	17	18
Parts/Process	Parts/Process	Parts/Process	Parts/Process	Parts/Process	Parts/Process	Parts/Process	Parts/Process	Parts/Process
Forecast / Plan	F & P	F & P	Control	Control	Control	Report / Review	R / R	R / R
Safety / Quality	Quantity	Time	Safety / Quality	Quantity	Time	Safety / Quality	Quantity	Time

The Products and Services Layer

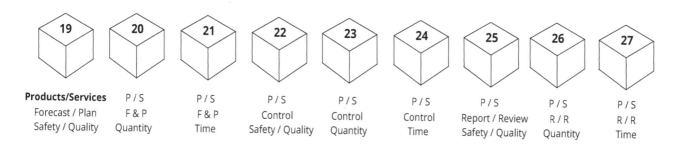

19	20	21	22	23	24	25	26	27
Products/Services	P / S	P / S	P / S	P / S	P / S	P / S	P / S	P / S
Forecast / Plan	F & P	F & P	Control	Control	Control	Report / Review	R / R	R / R
Safety / Quality	Quantity	Time	Safety / Quality	Quantity	Time	Safety / Quality	Quantity	Time

each of these Blocks ask the business owner or manager to think through the logical implications of the previous Block. So there becomes a chain of logical business thinking about improvements that allows the BI Leader and Team to work through their 'Idea' with a far greater understanding than most other techniques. Let's take an example:-

You're managing a Call Centre[17] with 30 team members, spread over 2 shifts of 12 hours each, working seven days a week. Your metrics show that one of your Teams (1 team leader and 5 members) are *performing* less well than their counterparts. Why?

The usual approach is to identify when that Team is next on shift, and then discuss the performance with their team leader: create an Action List to address the causes, make a note on their White Board, then monitor the situation to see if there is an improvement in performance. If not, then repeat these process steps. Compare this to the *'Business Cube'* approach.

We know that *'People'* are central: 'Process' could also be involved: 'Parts' are doubtful, and 'Service' is being negatively impacted. So the focus is clear. For *'Standards'*, then 'Safety' is marginal, but 'Quality', 'Quantity' and 'Time' are certainly involved. And the *'Management System'* metrics have indicated that one Team is under-performing, so we know the 'Reporting and Reviewing' element is working, but we're unsure about the 'Forecasting / Planning' and 'Controlling'. So let's lay out the **27 Blocks** in the **'Cube'**.

You will notice that many of the Blocks appear to be very similar: they are not. Each one is quite distinct, and that will become clear as we examine our Call Centre through the *'Business Cube'* approach. Starting with Block 1, note all the factors that you believe are impacting performance and involve 'People', 'Forecasting / Planning' and 'Safety / Quality'. Here are some of the common reasons:-

Team leader skills, management style, tactical and technical capabilities, lack of communication. Team member skill-sets, training and development, scripting.

Team hours worked, overtime, shift scheduling, allowances.
Reward system.
Forecasting: accuracy, freeze times, lead-time, time-frame.
Planning: short-term, variable, uncontrolled.
Safety: poor layout, non-compliant fire systems / procedures, over-crowding.
Quality: Equipment under specification, breakdowns, poor electrical supply.

These are a few of the possible factors: and a discussion with the Team Leader may be insightful, but it will never be comprehensive. At most, a Leader will focus on the 'Top 3' issues on their hit-list. So we move to Block 2, repeating the same methodology, except that 'Safety/Quality' has been replaced by 'Quantity'. And there's a list of possible factors:-

The work plan is under-estimating call traffic volumes.
Team members are poorly scheduled to handle these volumes
Call volumes peak at unpredictable times - which leads into the last element, 'Time'

By now, you are beginning to understand our approach to any Business Improvement. It is holistic, as well as is in detail. So you can understand the 'big picture', and the detail behind the picture. And the detail is split into two interwoven elements: the **Tactical** and the **Technical**. Tactical details are the people-focused issues - be they individual or team. Technical details are the 'numbers' - these impact every Block in the **'Business Cube'**, and are the bedrock of any business.

So the 'Cube' approach is very different to a traditional approach to 'Improvement' projects. The focus is on **structured thinking within a framework**, with the framework comprising of one Cube, three Layers and twenty seven Blocks: from the 'Big Picture' to the 'Details'.

Time to check your understanding so far:-

QUESTIONS - **BUSINESS CUBE**

Now there are **27 Blocks** centred around **RESOURCES, STANDARDS** and **MANAGEMENT SYSTEMS.**

Q1. Name the elements in the 1st. Block. _____

Q2. Why is Forecasting / Planning important for a Call Centre? _____

Q3. Why does Safety / Quality apply to people working in a Call Centre ? _____

Q4. Name the last of the elements in 'Standards' _____

Q5. Which element follows 'Forecasting / Planning? _____

Q6. How many Blocks are inside the 'Cube'? _____

So how did you do? If you managed to correctly answer five out of six, I'd be impressed. The Cube is a very different approach to the current thinking about business improvement. There's not an organization chart in sight: the same applies for Departments. Now you just use the 27 Blocks to prompt the questions that drive your business improvements. And those questions are in a structured sequence (because the *Cube is about structured thinking*), so the answers will emanate in a structured sequence, *providing you start at Block 1.* Before explaining the four *Rules of the Cube*, let's take a moment to understand what we're doing and why we're doing it.

If you think you've already identified an Improvement opportunity in your business, then identify the Blocks involved, and *think through the benefits and potential problems, starting at Block 1.* This process will help to *kill assumptions*, like 'I thought we had enough skilled people', and substitute them for facts. So we are *quantifying* all of the issues that could impact our Improvement, instead of a few of our preconceptions and a lot of other peoples' opinions. This approach will provide us with many of the facts to prepare our *Business Case for Improvement.*

If you're the *Boss*, and you don't have a clue where the Improvements could be, then *listen* to *Doll No. 4*, the Supervisors: they'll clarify the opportunities for their areas and provide a few hints as to where to look next in the business. Whether it's containing a current problem, or seizing an opportunity for Improvement, listen and then quantify in a structured way.

True Story: The opening of the £15bn Crossrail[18] line across London will be delayed by up to a year, it has been announced, after months of rumours that the engineering scheme was facing increasing difficulties. (The Guardian newspaper, 31st August 2018). London Crossrail opening postponed until autumn next year says a spokesman for £15bn project says it will miss its planned December 2018 opening date.

Crossrail project making good progress as plan to complete the railway is implemented - the central section of the Elizabeth line remains on schedule to open between October 2020 and March 2021. (The Crossrail website, 19th August 2019)

....This follows an update after the July [2020] Board [meeting] where it was announced that the central section could not open in summer 2021. (The Crossrail website, 21st August 2020). The latest cost estimate presented to the Board shows that the cost to complete the Crossrail project could be up to £1.1bn above the Financing Package agreed in December 2018 (£450m more than the upper end of the range announced in November 2019). **Work is ongoing to finalise the cost estimates.**

The Crossrail Project was aimed at reducing commuter travel times across London: the customer is 'Transport for London' (TfL), and the benefits are for many businesses and individuals who need to travel across London. I submit that an effective 'Cube' approach could have discovered the inherent flaws missed by using a traditional Agile Project methodology for a vastly complex engineering and logistical project. Fortunately, most of your Improvements will be nowhere near as complex: but the **same structured thinking can apply to small Improvements as well.**

True Story: A software upgrade for the new Boeing 737 MAX jetliner: could it get much smaller? The MCAS (Manoeuvring Characteristics Augmentation System) software was designed to compensate for performance deficiencies created by re-positioning the engines on each wing. The 'driver' for this business improvement was the reduction of the plane's operating costs by improving engine fuel efficiency. Following two fatal 737 MAX plane crashes in October 2018 and March 2019, the aircraft type was grounded. I submit that a 'Cube' approach would have benefited all stakeholders, not least the 346 passengers and crew who died in both accidents.

Exactly the same 'Cube' logic applies to the 'Parts and Process' Layer - and the 'Products and Services' Layer as well. The internal questions raised by each Block originate from the Improvement under consideration. So 'Parts' would probably provoke questions about the Supply Chain: 'Process' might lead to a more realistic Takt Time and balanced manufacturing process. The same logic for 'Products and Services': again, the reasoning is simple.

You change one Component in any given area, and there will be a consequent effect for other Blocks. This is not always understood: and the business ramifications for other areas can be misunderstood. This is partly due to business 'compartmentalization' - encouraged by Departments, Teams and anything that segments your business into 'parts'. So your customers don't experience a business or brand, they get the Customer Services Department, or Customer Care, or Customer Relationship Management. Remember: in terms of Improvements, the business is a complete entity, not a series of hurdles.

Instead of facing a series of hurdles, **the Cube uses three simple Rules.**

1. There's only **one Cube for any Business Unit**. That Unit may be the whole company, a division of the company, or a discrete entity within a business. Preferably, it's the whole business.

2. There are always three Layers and twenty seven Blocks in any Business Cube: they run sequentially, and never change.

3. Wherever you think your Improvement lies within the Cube, always start thinking at Block 1, working progressively through to Block 27. Please don't skip a Block or two. Make a note of all the factors that could impact your Improvement, and all the business elements that could be impacted by your Improvement. And take your time when doing this.

Experience has taught me that time spent thinking about the Improvement before it gets under-way can save a lot of wasted time and effort during the Improvement. Hence the title of this book, **'Think Twice, Cut Once'**. The Business Improvement Plan is part of the Business Cube. This Plan is generated after all the Cube Blocks have been considered, and all the relevant points noted. Historically, the Plan is one of the first elements created by the BI Team: with the Business Cube process, the Plan is prepared **after the Cube Blocks are completed.** It's an output of the Team's structured thinking. In case there's a doubt in the reader's mind, let's take a recent example of an excellent Business Improvement Project. Quoting from the British Medical Journal [bmj.com/content/369/bmj.m2025]. *"What the military do so well is planning for huge surges, because that's in the nature of their challenges. In the health service we tend to plan new services or service changes over months or years; engagement with patients and other service users takes time."* Because the changes in demand are mostly gradual—population ageing, for example—this time can be available. By contrast, planning for sudden, fast moving events like epidemics is the military's stock in trade. "They spend their lives* working through unexpected scenarios. The NHS[19] does have major incident plans, and every so often they're rehearsed. But this [the COVID pandemic] is on a rather different scale. Mark Norton, a former lieutenant colonel in the British army, talks of a distinctive **"philosophy of planning" that puts an emphasis on process.** "The process of planning is what's important rather than the actual plan as an output," he says. This perhaps counter-intuitive conclusion is a consequence of what Norton refers to as the great truism of military planning: **"that no plan survives contact with the enemy".** Military planning thus emphasises the **continual gathering of intelligence that might prompt changes to a plan.** Norton comments, **"It's a different philosophy to the one I've encountered in business, where a plan is usually made at the beginning of the year, and then you just work it through.** I say, for each patient I will need a 15 square metre cubicle with a ventilator and oxygen and this equipment in a trolley—and their expertise is scaling that up to 300, 500, whatever patients. They are bringing the logistical support for that to happen at incredible speed. I'm used to working in the NHS where to build a hospital is 15 years of planning. This has been done in 15 days. And if you have forgotten something or made an error, they are not phased at all: **the attitude is one of problem solving not blame. "They are very good at just making it happen; they don't go away and debate it and have committee meetings.** They take the instruction and operationalise that for you at great speed."

In this example, project leadership is very clear: everybody knows who the project manager is. Planning moves away from being static and inflexible towards more of a process - and that introduces the last aspect of the Business Cube. Once you've completed the Cube Blocks - all 27 - there's a need to regularly update the Cube details. A quick review means spending about 15 minutes on a late Tuesday and Thursday afternoons to update the progress of a BI at a medium-sized business: that's a BI involving between 3 and 6 active team members. This review is critical to ensure that the BI Plan, which is derived from the Business Cube, is **aligned** with the agreed Business Improvement objectives and the current operational status. And that taps into a **'different philosophy'**.

The Business Cube reflects the whole business, and inside the Cube sits the BI and the BI Plan, and there's a continual check to ensure that the Plan still fits the business needs, and that the BI itself is still fits the overall business goals. Once the **effectiveness** of the BI is assured, then assess the **efficiency** of the BI, starting with the Plan [Effectiveness is 'doing the right thing': efficiency is 'doing the thing right']. These two criteria are frequently blurred, and they are critically different. By stepping back and looking at the whole business, it's easier to spot any business improvement **'Creep'**, where the BI deliverables start to stretch the current BI Plan. Again, the Business Cube compels the BI Team to make that assessment against the 27 Blocks - not against the Plan. And there are plenty of software project planning Tools in the marketplace that perform this task semi-automatically; in my opinion, the ease with which these Tools can be used is part of the problem when managing business improvements: they circumvent the need for critically thinking of actual BI progress versus the Plan.

True Stories: New BI, new plan, and the first completed week of the assignment. And there's growing evidence that there's something 'wrong' with the Plan. After discussion with a few senior members of the BI Team, there's a 'revelation' - 'We're doing the wrong project' says one of the Directors. Fortunately, this was picked up after only one week, and it could be corrected without too much embarrassment.

Different project, a decade later: after completing the first week of the assignment, there's a realization that three out of five key areas for Improvement were unaware that we were starting the Improvement in that week. So easy question for the Project Manager: 'when was the last time we updated the CEO?'. The reply, 'Oh, about a month ago'. Not surprising that key managers were unaware of what was happening.

Both these examples are a typical BI 'disconnect': here the BI is disconnected from the whole business, and from the Plan, and that's before you starting comparing 'Planned Actions' against 'Actual' actions. There is a lack of alignment from the start of the BI. The Cube allows to check your activities against the whole business and the BI, then the BI against the Plan, and then Plan against Actual activities. It's a tiered approach, top to bottom, from the 'Big Picture' to the 'Detail' if required.

This is how the 'military' managers used their Hospital Plan: this is one of the key reasons why this BI was so successful. The second reason was the clear leadership demonstrated, and it's ability to 'cut through the bureaucracy' of the usual hospital construction process.

These are the basics that you need to start using this approach for business improvements. Before progressing to the next section, let's find out how you did with the six questions. If you were correct with 5 out of the 6, then I'd be impressed.

Answers to Questions 1 to 6

1. People, Forecast / Plan, Safety / Quality.
2. Need to know the number of People required to handle a given volume of Calls.
3. Safety of your people is paramount: Quality of their working environment impacts productivity and performance for individuals and teams.
4. Time.
5. Control.
6. 27 - unlike a traditional Rubik Cube, which has 26.

Business Improvements

In this diagram, we show the four drivers of effective business improvements: leadership, systems and then structured thinking, and lastly neuro-linguistic programming[20] (NLP) and the logical levels model[21] (LLM). The 29 Tools are the 'levers' you select to deliver the business benefits.

The Business Cube approach is both a System and Process that promotes creative thinking about BI in a structured format that everybody can read and understand

3. Structured Thinking about Business Improvements

Type in 'Structured Thinking' on the internet, and see what pops up. Here are three postings:-

Structured thinking is a process of putting a framework to an unstructured problem. 'Having a structure not only helps a [business] analyst understand the problem at a macro level, it also helps by identifying areas which require deeper understanding'. (Analytics Vidhya[22])

Structured Thinking and Communication is one of the most important skill data science managers and customers value today. *Sadly, there aren't many resources which help people in this area.* This course was created with an aim to address this need and provide people with frameworks and best practices on structured thinking and communications. Specifically, we will teach:
1. How to take ambiguous business problems and then break them into structured data science problems.
2. How to present your analysis and business insights in an impactful manner.
3. How to do clear and structured written communications which people can easily understand.
(Analytics Vidhya)

Structured Thinking: Bringing Consistency to Problem Management
'Structured (or convergent) thinking can organize a flood of information to reveal suspicious gaps in data, bringing efficiency and speed to problem investigation. Using a consistent approach focused on critical data coupled with a visual representation of this thinking tremendously improves communication and collaboration. Besides significantly advancing the search for true root cause'. (Kepner-Tregoe[23])

Three postings about Structured Thinking. While there is some content in the marketplace, I'll re-iterate the second line of the second quote: *'Sadly, there aren't many resources which help people in this area':* **True.**

The Business Cube is specifically designed for this segment of the business tool market. It provides a framework for Structured Thinking. It's a Tool with Rules that has been proven to work for over a dozen Business Improvement assignments. And the benefits are significant:-

1. Improved understanding of business improvements at both the macro- and micro-level.
2. Logical, sequential business analysis that can be tracked: the Cube places the 'People Layer' first, starting with Safety/Quality - do you think this happened with the 737 MAX upgrade?
3. See the Business Links through the Cube - understand how people, activities and processes are really connected.
4. Focus on value-added activities and costs: know your business drivers and Improvement bottlenecks before meeting them head-on.

Because there are few comparable tools currently available, it's difficult to make direct assessments with other products: here are some offerings in a random order:-

Structured Thinking: The Pyramid Principle[24] - Barbara Minto - The McKinsey Approach[25]
Theory of Change[26] - ActKnowledge
'Structured thinking' is about building a big answer by asking many small questions - N. Goke
Unified Structured Inventive Thinking (USIT) is a structured, problem-solving methodology.
Systematic Inventive Thinking[27] **(SIT)** is a thinking method.
MECE (Mutually Exclusive, Collectively Exhaustive) is a systematic problem-solving framework that helps to solve complex business problems.
Solving Complex Problems: Structured Thinking, Design Principles, and AI - core principles that will change the way you approach and solve large-scale challenges.
The art of structured thinking and analyzing[28] - K. Jain - who explains in some detail the benefits of structured thinking. *I have started thinking in a structured manner. I have gained experience in best data management practices. My business thinking has evolved over time. While the last two points improve only with time, structured thinking can improve quickly through simple training and disciplined approach towards analysis. But before we go forward, let me bring out the benefits from structured thinking through following graph:*

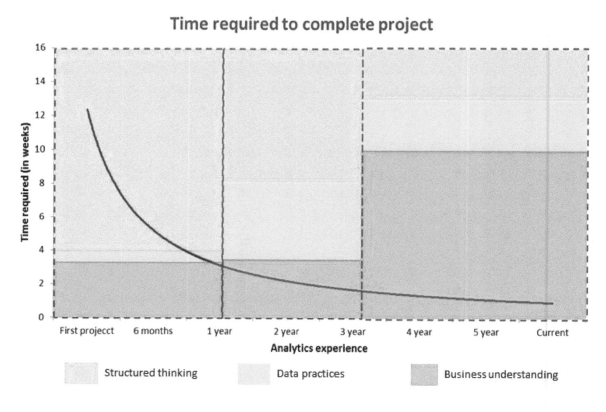

Fig. 6: Structured Thinking and BI Project Benefits.

*Here is how to read this graph: Red line in the graph shows how time to complete a project (in weeks) has come down with experience. Within each of three blocks (< 1 year; 1 – 3 year; 3+ years), the area of colour shows the factor responsible for drop in time. For example, during the first block, **time required to complete the project comes down from 12+ weeks to 3 weeks and 75% of this drop is because of structured thinking.** As you can see, structured thinking is a a big differentiator between a good analyst and bad analyst. Not only this, you cannot become a good analytics manager until you can put structure to complex and ambiguous problems. Hence, this post is aimed to help you progress on the path of structured thinking.* My work experience is in operations management and business improvement, and we sometimes

20

use Analytics at the start of assignments. Apart from that, there are close similarities in our work: the main difference is that it took me about *10 years to achieve a drop from 12+ weeks to 3*. And it was structured thinking that allowed me to deliver a proposed 4 week business analysis in Argentina in 1 week. So let's recap the 'Cube' structure before looking at what's **inside** the Blocks.

Layer 1 - People - Starting at Block 1, consider all aspects of your proposed Improvement that could involve People. This covers employees, contractors, the five Dolls and suppliers, plus any future hires. Think lead-times for specialists: you can't expect to recruit and select the best candidates in less than 4 weeks: usually takes 6 months! This is where the organization chart can be quite deceptive. *True Story:* Organization charts for Chinese owned businesses are normally well-documented: the real organization will revolve around the owner's family members.

Layer 2 - Parts and Process - Begins at Block 10, and covers the whole supply chain, plus all their contractors. Usually an interlinked spider's web, often with computer systems that don't talk with each other. *True Story:* Understand your supplier's costing structure for all parts, even if they protest it got nothing to do with you.

Layer 3 - Products and Services - Block 19, using the same criteria to assess the Improvement, before making any Plans. Use all the Blocks to flush out inconsistencies in the proposed Improvement: to firstly align the Layers, then all the Blocks in the Layers, ensuring that everything relevant has been thought of and accounted for. Working with a Team chosen from different areas of the business is essential. *True Story:* Never make assumptions about the product: sometimes it's been deliberately designed not to work!

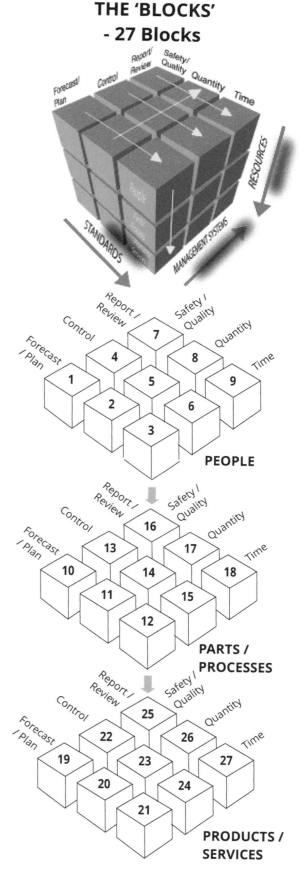

THE 'BLOCKS'
- 27 Blocks

PEOPLE

PARTS /
PROCESSES

PRODUCTS /
SERVICES

Once you've understood the concept of 'Layers' (useful when explaining to the Boss about how the Cube works), then moving to Blocks is relatively simple. Only the 'People' element has layers: 'Standards' and 'Management Systems' remain constant.

True Story: Years ago, I tried 'layering' management systems. Taking the then popular themes of World-Class Manufacturing, Advanced Manufacturing and Basic Manufacturing, I split a typical list of management reporting tools into these three categories before presenting at an internal management meeting. Huge mistake! The Director chairing the meeting commented, 'I don't know which textbook you got this out of….', and that was where the discussion began and ended. Never again did I discuss any thoughts on the development of business improvement methodologies.

Using the Blocks in the Cube sequence offers the best approach to positioning the business improvement Tools (BITs) that are available. Let me explain. There are hundreds of BITs out there supporting a huge industry. *'UK's management consulting industry grew by 7% last year to breach the £10 billion mark for the first time. The industry's headcount in the country meanwhile topped 60,000 consultants, as many firms ramped up their capabilities to meet a spike in consulting demand'.* And that is only in the UK! Admittedly, these figures are pre-COVID, so there'll be a slump in demand and revenue in 2020: but even allowing for this, it remains a profitable market.

If you're thinking about improving your business performance, then which Tool is best suited for what you want to achieve? If you're the Boss, the chances are you'll know somebody who can advise you on the best Tools available. For a manufacturing process improvement, it could be 'Lean Six Sigma' - popular, proven, and fit-for-purpose. But is the opportunity to improve the manufacturing process aligned with all your other functions? - can Sales find more customers at the current margins to sell the increased volume of product that you're aiming to produce? And would you really invest in a Tool on the recommendation of business friends and associates? The answer is 'Yes'.

That's how most business improvements are actually conceived: it's somebody's idea (usually the Boss), which is then defined, measured and analyzed (DMAIC)[29], before being executed. Too late to change your mind at that stage!

The Cube approach is different. Before any business improvement moves from 'Idea' to 'Define', **use the Cube discipline to evaluate the Improvement impact on your business as a**

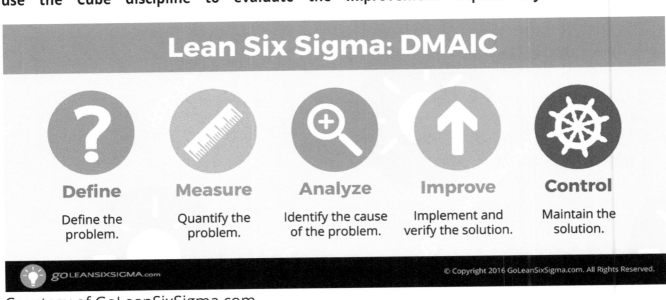

Courtesy of GoLeanSixSigma.com

whole. I'm reminded of Stephen Covey's[30] '7 Habits of Highly Successful people', and Habit number 5, *'Seek first to understand, then to be understood'*. The Cube is a framework and discipline to understand the impact of Improvements on your business before embarking on any radical changes. The only business health warning is that it will do 'no harm' - only make you think logically and comprehensively about the consequences of your Business Improvement decisions.

We've mentioned one BIT - 'Lean Six Sigma', which can become more of a doctrine than a Tool. There are many others. I've listed 29 Tools that I've used over a 35 year timespan, and they have all been effective at delivering business Improvements. They're included in the 'Blocks and Tools' figure below. They are not in order of importance, or preference, or business-impact: they are in

[Blocks and Tools - in Layers, then Blocks, against the 29 BI Tools in the Toolkit[30]].

BLOCKS AND TOOLS

Resources	People									Parts & Process									Products & Services								
Management Systems	Forecast / Plan			Control			Report/Review			Forecast / Plan			Control			Report / Review			Forecast & Plan			Control			Report / Review		
Standards	S/Q	Q	T	S/Q	Q	T	S/Q	Q	T	S/Q	Q	T	S/Q	Q	T	S/Q	Q	T	S/Q	Q	T	S/Q	Q	T	S/Q	Q	T
Tools \ Blocks	1	2	3	4	5	6	7	8	9	10	11	12	13	14	15	16	17	18	19	20	21	22	23	24	25	26	27
Recruitment & Selection																											
Reward Triangle																											
Training & Development																											
Activity Based Costing																											
Master Schedule																											
Social Media																											
Lean Six Sigma																											
Total Quality Management																											
Takt Time																											
Load Balance																											
Design for Manufacture																											
Kaizen Flow																											
Kaizen Process																											
Information Systems																											
Self-Directed Work Teams																											
Single Minutes Exchange of Dies																											
Just-in-Time																											
Margin Control																											
Hoshin Kanri																											
Kaikaku																											
Capacity Release																											
Waterfall Projects																											
Agile Projects																											
Artificial Intelligence																											
Radio Frequency Identification																											
Real Time Location Systems																											
KPIs / Balanced Scorecard																											
Margins																											
Cash Control																											

'Cube' sequence. Starting at Block 1, run your eye down the first column, where there are 29 Tools. They might be unknown to you, or you might have heard of some of them, but there are 6 tools that are applicable to Block 1. That means that they can influence the business in the 'People', 'Forecast / Plan', and 'Safety / Quality' Block. So the Cube indicates certain tools could be useful.

True Story: I've witnessed a seance used to try and communicate with 'business' spirits: and a ouija board to help with recruitment and selection decisions. I think the Cube approach is a definite improvement!

So the same logic applies to the remaining Blocks: and this is a subjective view for both the Tools in the list, and the Blocks that they influence. For example, if you take 'Social Media', then you can see that it doesn't apply to the 'Parts and Process' element. But then there are examples of manufacturing processes being used to promote the efficacy of a business' products and services, such as car production (Mercedes) or alcoholic drinks (Guinness). Social media can promote your business: or it can be used to denigrate your business. Be careful here - so it gets crossed off my list

THE 'BLOCKS'
- 27 Blocks

PEOPLE

PARTS & PROCESSES

PRODUCTS & SERVICES

29 TOOLS

ALIGNING BLOCKS & TOOLS

Tool	Block Nos.
Recruitment & Selection	1 - 9
Reward Triangle	1 - 9
Training & Development	4 - 24
Activity Based Costing	4 - 24
Master Schedule	4 - 24
Social Media	4 - 9, 10 -24
Lean Six Sigma	4 - 27
TQM (Total Quality Mgt.)	4 - 29
Takt Time	1 - 27
Load Balance	4 - 18
DFM (Design for Manufacture)	10 - 27
Kaizen (Flow)	10 - 24
Kaizen (Process)	10 - 24
Information Systems	1 - 27
SDWTs (self-Directed Work Teams)	4 - 24
SMEDs (Single Minutes Exchange of Dies)	10 - 18
JIT (Just-In-Time)	10 - 27
Margin Control	10 - 27
Hoshin Kanri	10 - 18
Kaikaku (Sudden Impact)	4 - 27
Capacity Release	4 - 24
Waterfall Projects	4 - 27
Agile Projects	4 - 27
AI (Artificial Intelligence)	4 - 27
RFID (Radio Frequency Identification)	10 - 27
RTLS (Real Time Location Systems)	4 - 27
KPIs., Balanced scorecard	1 - 27
Margins	4 - 27
Cash control	1 - 27

Now it's unlikely that you're aware of all the tools in the list. And the simple fact is that business improvement Leaders and Teams get most excited about the 'new' skills and techniques they're going to learn on their next assignment. Which is not surprising, but it does deflect from focusing on the key objective - achieving the business benefits: and then it becomes clearer as to why there's a continuing need for the Boss. As the management consulting marketplace is estimated to be worth $295b. by 2020, it's a rapidly growing industry in itself: and there's a smorgasbord of BITs that always seem to be just what your business needs to use to improve. Before opting for the latest or most popular Tools, use the Cube approach to understand your business needs in more detail, and the likely impact of any BI on your whole business . There's a multitude of tools available, and here's a rough guide to the **effort** required to implement them and the level of **impact** on the performance of your business:-

Low Effort / High Impact
Social Media
Takt Time
DFM (Design for Manufacturing)
Load Balance
RFID (Radio Frequency Identification)
RTLS (Real Time Location Systems)
Margin Control
Margins
Cash Control
KPIs / Balanced Scoreboard
Capacity Release

High Effort / High Impact
Recruitment & Selection
Training & Development
Activity Based Costing
Master Schedule
Lean Six Sigma
TQM (Total Quality Management)
JIT (Just-in-Time)
Kaizen (Flow)
Kaizen (Process)
SDWTs (Self Directed Work Teams)
Kaikaku
Agile Projects
SMEDs (Single Minutes Exchange of Dies)

Low Effort / Low Impact
Reward triangle

High Effort / Low Impact
Information systems
Waterfall Projects
AI (Artificial Intelligence)
Hoshin Kanri

The above are tools that I've used over the decades, and this assessment is based on my personal experience. I'm not qualified to comment on other Tools. So the 29 Tools listed are not being promoted over tools: it's more about getting the reader to think through their use and the impact of their use.

For those who are new to business improvement, it's useful to briefly describe these tools. For those of you who are professional business consultants or experienced BI practitioners, then you can skip this Chapter, and move to 'Using the Cube', which gives some practical examples of the Cube in a live business environment. And for those who enjoy some *true stories*, you can just read the blue-lined sentences in the next section to keep you amused!

So here goes - the most effective 29 business improvements that I can vouch for..........

4. Twenty Nine Tools

1.   Recruitment & Selection - One of the most critical of all the tools, and one of the most problematic. Often the root of many issues for all types of businesses, and still a highly subjective area of business management. My advice: clarify your thinking by asking the simple question: what behaviours does this business reward people for? Is it their work performance, their personality, or their ability to cope with the political aspects of their workplace? Once you've understood this, focus on re-aligning the process towards the 'Performance' factor - the lack of business performance is probably why you're undertaking a BI in the first place. And if you're looking for inspiration, check out the three hiring questions that Jeff Bezos (Founder and CEO of Amazon.com Inc.) noted in his 1998 'Letter to Shareholders'.

Q1.   Will you admire this person?
Q2.   Will this person raise the average level of effectiveness of the group they're entering?
Q3.   Along what dimension might this person be a superstar?

True Story: The subject of my MBA thesis many decades ago was my employer's recruitment and selection process for managers. Before submitting my work, I gave a copy to our HR Department, who passed on a copy to the Boss. Nobody read it, until one day the IT manager picked up the HR copy. A few hour's later, the Boss's copy vanished from his desk, and nothing further was said. So you can complete a MBA, just be careful of the topic you choose.

2.   Reward Triangle[32] - Just draw a triangle on a whiteboard, label the three corners 'Performance', 'Personality' and 'Politics', and ask each member of the audience (least senior first) to place a 'x' on how they believe they are rewarded at work. In every case, you'll find 'Personality' and 'Politics' outweigh 'Performance' - and that's how a constructive workshop on individual and team performance improvement can start. Simple approach, not in any previous textbook, and can be used at any organizational level in the business.

True Story: Based on a Senior Management workshop where the two top Bosses kept arguing with me. One Boss had a 'Sales' background, the other was from 'Finance': so I posed a simple question. 'Do relationships build results or results build relationship?' Once they'd started arguing between themselves, instead of with me, we were able to shift the agenda to the Reward Triangle, and identify some performance improvements that would lead to better business results.

3.   Training and Development - Often one of the cornerstones of the Human Resources function, and probably not aligned with the requirements of future business improvements. There can be issues with the General Data Protection Regulation (GDPR), which introduced new rules for organizations that offer goods and services to people in the European Union (EU), or who collected and analyzed data for EU residents no matter where you or your enterprise are located. Once aware of these legal complexities, then it is vital that the BI Leader and Team work closely with the HR Team. In the hierarchy of the Russian Dolls, the head of HR is definitely a No.2, along with the heads of

Finance, Sales/Marketing and Operations. Involve them whenever practical, and ensure they are in lock-step with the Improvements.

True Story: Training and development of people in any business is a 'contact' activity, even in a post-COVID world! If you're expecting behaviour to improve through reading a manual, or completing an on-line test, then expect a long wait. We doubled line productivity in less than a week using the Single Piece Flow technique for one assembly business: the management team were sceptical, so we trained them, placed them on the assembly line, and they replicated the performance. Think this: Involve, train, do, practice, improve performance.

The bad news: *The number of skills required for a single job is increasing by 10% year over year, and over 30% of the skills needed three years ago will soon be irrelevant, according to Gartner TalentNeuron™ data analysis [2020] on millions of job postings. The lack of digital skills is already apparent and the pace of change is leaving HR - and employees - playing catch-up.*

4. **Activity Based Costing (ABC)** - Probably the most underestimated BIT of all. In terms of cost accounting, this approach matches costs with activities that cause and create those costs. So products and services consume activities, and its activities that consume resources: activities become the cost drivers. 'ABC' is part of Activity Based Management, which enables management to better understand how and where the business makes a profit, and where the money is spent, and where the greatest potential for cost reductions are. However you decide to measure the business's cost base, **understand your costs in detail.**

MASTER SCHEDULE 2018 – 2021

Rev £K.		April	May	June	July	August	Sept	Oct	Nov	Dec	Jan	Feb	March	Target % +
	2017	30	31	31	45	40	55	45	45	28	58	44	49	1
	2018	34	46	74	64	103	74	61	61	38	78	59	66	1.35
	2019	41	55	89	77	124	89	73	73	45	94	71	66	1.20
	2020	53	72	115	100	161	116	95	95	59	122	93	79	1.30
	2021	61	83	133	115	185	133	109	109	68	140	107	119	1.15

PEOPLE PLAN 2018 – 21

	No. of FTEs.	April	May	June	July	August	Sept	Oct	Nov	Dec	Jan	Feb	March	Target Rev. per Employee
						FULL TIME EQUIVALENT GUIDELINE								
2017	ACTUAL	7	7	7	7	7	7	7	7	7	7	7	7	
	Rev. per Employee	4.3	4.4	4.4	6.4	5.7	7.9	6.4	6.4	4.0	8.3	6.3	7.0	6.5
2018	ACTUAL / PLAN	7	7	7	8	8	8	7	7	4	9	7	8	
	Rev. per Employee	4.9	6.6	10.6	8.0	12.9	8.8	8.8	8.8	8.8	8.8	8.8	8.8	8.8
2019	PLAN	5	7	11	10	16	11	9	9	6	12	9	10	
	Rev. per Employee	7.8	7.8	7.8	7.8	7.8	7.8	7.8	7.8	7.8	7.8	7.8	7.8	7.8
2020	PLAN	5	6	10	9	14	10	8	8	5	11	8	9	
	Rev. per Employee	11.4	11.4	11.4	11.4	11.4	11.4	11.4	11.4	11.4	11.4	11.4	11.4	11.4
2021	PLAN	7	9	15	13	21	15	12	12	8	16	12	13	
	Rev. per Employee	9.0	9.0	9.0	9.0	9.0	9.0	9.0	9.0	9.0	9.0	9.0	9.0	9.0

True Story: Working through the cost base of a product services business, it was discovered that many customers were being served at an operating loss - there was no profit being made from the work undertaken. Quotes supplied to potential customers always showed a profit: when the job was completed, the margin had reduced!

5. **Master Schedule**[33] **(MS)** - Translates a business plan into a comprehensive product manufacturing schedule that covers what is to be assembled or made, when, with what materials acquired and when, and the cash required. Whether your business is large, small or medium-sized, an effective MS can be prepared without too much difficulty. But it does require a disciplined approach to costings and revenue projections: a certain realism about actual costs and realistic revenues. if you're

the Boss, then get involved: don't leave this to the accountant or book-keeper. Understand how the numbers are being calculated, where the data is coming from, and who is responsible. And forecast at least 12 months ahead, allowing you to plan people, parts and cash-flow. Cash planning and control is the 29th Tool in the list - last, but still very important.

SALES & MARKETING PLAN 2021

		% Margin	April	May	June	July	August	Sept	Oct	Nov	Dec	Jan	Feb	March	Mid-point	Target
		%	%	%	%	%	%	%	%	%	%	%	%	%	%	%
Zone 1	New	35	35	35	35	35	35	35	35	35	35	35	35	35	35	35
	Service	35	36	36	36	36	36	36	36	36	36	36	36	36	36	35
Zone 2	New	32	28	28	28	28	28	28	28	28	28	28	28	28	28	30
	Service	30	28	28	28	28	28	28	28	28	28	28	28	28	28	30
Zone 3	New	30	15	15	15	15	15	15	15	15	15	15	15	15	15	15
	Service	30	15	15	15	15	15	15	15	15	15	15	15	15	15	15
Zone 4	New	26	10	10	10	10	10	10	10	10	10	10	10	10	10	10
	Service	24	10	10	10	10	10	10	10	10	10	10	10	10	10	10
Zone 5	New	24	5	5	5	5	5	5	5	5	5	5	5	5	6	6
	Service	24	5	5	5	5	5	5	5	5	5	5	5	5	6	6
Zone 6	New	24	5	5	5	5	5	5	5	5	5	5	5	5	6	6
	Service	24	5	5	5	5	5	5	5	5	5	5	5	5	6	6
	Total New		98	98	98	98	98	98	98	98	98	98	98	98		
	Total Service		99	99	99	99	99	99	99	99	99	99	99	99	Total £K	%Growth
Rev £K.	2017		30	31	31	45	40	55	45	45	28	58	44	49	501	
	2018		34	46	74	52	46	63	52	52	32	55	55	60	621	15%
	2019		41	55	89	62	55	76	62	62	39	66	66	72	745	20%
	2020		53	72	115	81	72	99	81	81	50	86	86	94	968	30%
	2021		65	83	133	93	83	113	93	93	58	99	99	108	1118	15%

BUSINESS PLAN 2021

		% Split	£	£	£	£	£	£	£	£	£	£	£	£	Total £K
Zone 1	New	0.80	18.2	23.1	37.2	26.0	23.1	31.8	26.0	26.0	16.2	27.6	27.6	30.1	312.9
	Service	0.20	4.7	5.9	9.6	6.7	5.9	8.2	6.7	6.7	4.2	7.1	7.1	7.8	80.5
Zone 2	New	0.85	15.5	19.6	31.6	22.1	19.6	27.0	22.1	22.1	13.7	23.5	23.5	25.6	266.0
	Service	0.15	2.7	3.5	5.6	3.9	3.5	4.8	3.9	3.9	2.4	4.1	4.1	4.5	46.9
Zone 3	New	0.85	8.3	10.5	16.9	11.8	10.5	14.5	11.8	11.8	7.4	12.6	12.6	13.7	142.5
	Service	0.15	1.5	1.9	3.0	2.1	1.9	2.6	2.1	2.1	1.3	2.2	2.2	2.4	25.1
Zone 4	New	0.85	5.5	7.0	11.3	7.9	7.0	9.6	7.9	7.9	4.9	8.4	8.4	9.1	95.0
	Service	0.15	1.0	1.2	2.0	1.4	1.2	1.7	1.4	1.4	0.9	1.5	1.5	1.6	16.8
Zone 5	New	0.85	2.8	3.5	5.6	3.9	3.5	4.8	3.9	3.9	2.5	4.2	4.2	4.6	47.5
	Service	0.15	0.5	0.6	1.0	0.7	0.6	0.9	0.7	0.7	0.4	0.7	0.7	0.8	8.4
Zone 6	New	0.85	2.8	3.5	5.6	3.9	3.5	4.8	3.9	3.9	2.5	4.2	4.2	4.6	47.5
	Service	0.15	0.5	0.6	1.0	0.7	0.6	0.9	0.7	0.7	0.4	0.7	0.7	0.8	8.4
	Total New		53.0	67.3	108.3	75.7	67.3	92.5	75.7	75.7	47.1	80.5	80.5	87.8	911.4
	Total Service		12.0	15.2	24.5	17.1	15.2	20.9	17.1	17.1	10.7	18.2	18.2	19.9	206.2

True Story: Working at a large manufacturing plant in the UK, they had installed new software to manage their Material Requirement Planning[34] (MRP). As a direct result, equipment was removed, people made redundant, and plant capacity reduced by 30%. Having just arrived on-site to deliver a Productivity Improvement Project (PIP), I decided to double-check the computer-generated demand requirement numbers and production plan. A basic 'paper and pencil' exercise showed that customer's demand would outstrip production rates within 8 weeks. The manufacturing plant was completely 'out-of-balance', between different work stations, machines, delivery schedules and raw material levels. The crisis required the following actions were taken immediately:-

1.   Re-calculate raw material requirements and bring forward deliveries.
2.   Take the abandoned equipment off the scrap heap, re-wire and rebuild it.
3.   Re-employ twelve people who had been made redundant.
4.   Re-balance the flow of work throughout the whole plant.

There are several lessons to be learnt here. Never trust a software-based system to generate accurate business numbers without doing a manual check first. Never make decisions on numbers you cannot trust: verify the numbers throughout the planning and delivery cycle. And always refer to the customer demand rate before calculating the 'Takt' time. Use a calculator with your paper and pencil!

6.   Social Media - Without doubt, this is the one Tool that has had the most impact on reshaping the commercial and business landscape over the past 30 years. Never underestimate the power of Social Media: leverage it at every opportunity. But remember, it 'cuts both ways'. The praise and enthusiasm that can be generated for your products and services can turn to biting criticism if your business fails to deliver the promised benefits. As you build your social strategy, utilize your influencers to create unique content for your brand and increase brand awareness. Listen to your audience to join relevant conversations already happening on social, and to guide your future social strategy. Compare your efforts with those of your competitors, track your content's performance on social, and adjust your content to align with the user at every stage of the sales funnel. A simple formula for measuring Return on Investment (RoI) from Social Media is:-

Revenue / investment (people hours, ad budget, etc.) X 100 = social media ROI (as a %)

True Story: At a weekly meeting of my local business group, a successful small business owner said,' I spend a lot of money on Social Media, but I haven't any idea what the return is'. Stop spending now! Use data analytics to understand exactly what your return on investment is before spending another penny.

7. Lean Six Sigma - By far the most famous BIT in the business marketplace. A marriage of 'Lean' thinking with 'Six Sigma' mechanics to eliminate the 8 types of 'Waste'[35]: Defects, Over-Production, Waiting, Skill's Waste, Transportation, Inventory, Motion, and Extra-Processing. Credit for coining the term Six Sigma goes to an engineer named Bill Smith who helped Motorola realize an estimated $16b. of savings during the 1980s as a result of standardizing core processes. Once you couple Lean and Six Sigma in one BI package, then it's an extremely powerful Improvement Tool, particularly for processes. But there is a downside. It produces a narrowness of business improvement thinking, a 'one Tool fits all problems' idea. So BI Leaders become focused on repeating the same business diagnosis using the same methodology: a 'more-of-the-same' mentality. There's a tendency to be blind-sided by business surprises. The outbreak of COVID-19 is an example.

True story: There have been major viral outbreaks in the world before, which have been contained closer to their source. So when I worked in the Far East, it was not unusual to wear gloves and a face-mask when working. Returning to Europe, when I mentioned COVID-19 at a Board Meeting in early 2020, the Chairman closed down the discussion. I've seen the same thinking applied to Lean Six Sigma: if you're not Lean Six Sigma trained and qualified, then some Bosses are reluctant to continue the conversation. So the tail starts to wag the dog: Lean Six Sigma looking for a business issue to fix or opportunity to seize. That is a positively dangerous approach for business improvement.

8. TQM (Total Quality Management) - More of a philosophy than a business tool, with an emphasis on:-
Customer-focus: The customer ultimately determines the level of quality.
Total employee involvement: All employees participate in working toward common goals. High-performance work systems integrate continuous improvement efforts with normal business operations. Self-directed work teams[36] are one form of empowerment.
Process-centred: A fundamental part of TQM is a focus on process thinking. A process is a series of steps that take inputs from suppliers (internal or external) and transforms them into outputs that are delivered to customers (internal or external).

Integrated system: Although an organization may consist of many different functional specialities often organized into vertically structured departments, it is the horizontal processes interconnecting these functions that are the focus of TQM. Micro-processes add up to larger processes, and all processes aggregate into the business processes required for defining and implementing strategy. Everyone must understand the vision, mission, and guiding principles as well as the quality policies, objectives, and critical processes of the organization. Business performance must be monitored and communicated continuously. An integrated system connects business improvement elements in an attempt to continually improve and exceed the expectations of customers, employees, and other stakeholders.

Strategic and systematic approach: A critical part of the management of quality is the strategic and systematic approach to achieving an organization's vision, mission, and goals. This process, called strategic planning or strategic management, includes the formulation of a strategic plan that integrates quality as a core component.

Continual improvement: A large aspect of TQM is continual process improvement. Continual improvement drives an organization to be both analytical and creative in finding ways to become more competitive and more effective at meeting stakeholder expectations.

Fact-based decision making: In order to know how well an organization is performing, data on performance measures are necessary. TQM requires that an organization continually collect and analyze data in order to improve decision making accuracy, achieve consensus, and allow prediction based on past history.

Communications: During times of organizational change effective communications plays a large part in maintaining morale and in motivating employees at all levels.

True Fact: As you may have guessed, TQM is my preferred tool for Business Improvement. It provides a set of beliefs that allow many other Tools to operate within its framework. And its applicable throughout the business.

9. 'Takt' Time - Adjustable time unit used in Lean production to synchronize the rate of production with the rate of demand. Keeping your finger on the pulse of product and service demand is absolutely critical. Whether this is a weekly or monthly check, or some other time period, depends on the customers' demand variations. This tool should be integrated with your MS and MRP[36] systems, so the impact of making adjustments on your supply chain is mitigated.

True Story: The Takt Time is rarely shown on any KPI (Key Performance Indicators) for a manufacturing plant. Sitting at the weekly meeting to agree next week's production requirements, I realised that the value of the proposed volumes was more than £1m., which greatly exceeded their present run-rate. Didn't occur to any of the senior team to check production plan against capacity against present rates.

10. Load Balance: This involves balancing the work rate between sub-processes in order to efficiently match customer demand or Takt time. Then the process is always on-time but never idle. Seems an obvious requirement in a production or process environment.

of Cube options. And if you'd prefer to think 'Cube', then the same information is laid out as below:-

True Story - The production Lines were fine-tuned to operate at optimum loadings: the problem was that breakdowns and stoppages were negating the benefit of 'Toyota-like' precision process flow. Moral of the story: get the manufacturing basics right before attempting anything sophisticated. And this type of problem is not confined to manufacturing. *Another client couldn't understand why there was so little cash in their business account. Looking at the flow of work, we discovered a bottleneck in the Accounts Receivable Department. Collecting all the cheques waiting to be paid in, and placing them in piles on the floor, the aggregate height was 13.5 feet.*

11. DFM (Design for Manufacture) is the process of designing parts, components or products for ease of manufacturing with an end goal of making a better product at lower cost. DFM needs to occur very early in the whole process.

True Story - A tale of 26 parts that didn't fit! Engineers had designed a camera where each of the 26 components did not come together: it was designed not to work. Why? There was a round of redundancies proposed when two manufacturing sites were being merged into one: to make sure that they weren't made redundant, this technically advanced camera was designed to fail. There were no immediate redundancies.

12. Kaizen Flow refers to the flow of information and materials through an entire 'Value System' – a value system is where there is added commercial value each process step of the way. And **Kaizen is a mentality,** a way of thinking about work that helps BI Teams practising it to eliminate waste, improve process flow or increase productivity (output per person per hour) increase value creation.

True Story - One medium-sized business was experiencing rapid sales growth, and their processes at every level were unable to cope with the product and service volumes. There had to be a complete overhaul of all their processes, and this had to be done in a few weeks – what happened was pure 'Kaikaku' – with an element of 'Skunk' works thrown in. (Lockheed and Kelly Johnson)

13. Kaizen Process - Japanese term (translated as 'the real place') for a gradual approach to ever higher standards in quality enhancement and waste reduction, through small but continual improvements **involving everyone from the chief executive to the lowest level workers.** And that's the benefits and the business problem! This Process is excellent, but gradual and incremental, which may not be at the rate of improvement required to deliver the BI. **Kaizen Process can run constantly in the background of your business, but please don't think that it will automatically provide the competitive edge that your business may urgently need.**

True Story: - Working with an Asset Management Company in the City of London and Canary Wharf, we found that they placed a sizeable sum of corporate cash on the overnight market (1). Which financial institution they placed the money with was the responsibility of the department secretary.

After a brief conversation, we discovered that there were only twelve possible institutions that were considered: they were the only ones the secretary had been given the telephone number for. When informed, the Managing Director only uttered two words: 'Good God'.

(1) The **overnight market** is the component of the money market involving the shortest term loan. Lenders agree to lend borrowers' funds only "overnight" (i.e. the borrower must repay the borrowed funds plus interest at the start of business the next day).

14. Information Systems are the software and hardware systems that support data-intensive applications. Like GDPR (General Data Protection Regulation) – written by lawyers and policy makers. See GDPR article.

True Story: A leading aircraft manufacturer was implementing a new ERP system, using skilled Team Members who were already employees. After 6 months, the Team had grown to 55 Members, and was diverting resources from other parts of the business. Then one manager discovered that you couldn't purchase an aircraft part without purchasing the whole aircraft: there were a number of fundamental flaws in the software configuration. The project was abandoned.

15. SDWTs[36] (Self Directed Work teams) – are groups of employees who manage themselves and their work. You give them the Tools, and they manage themselves! Seems like a management panacea, except that it requires a relatively stable workforce and the full support of the Boss. Mastering team dynamics is the key to success.

True Story: If you want to see the advantages and pitfalls of SDWTs., take a look at Call Centres. When working effectively, small groups of call handlers can manage their own time within the Team and deliver excellent customer service. Or they can appear to be doing exactly the same activities and deliver disastrous results for your business and customers. With SDWTs., the 'devil is in the detail' – they manage themselves, and you monitor them managing themselves. Have fun!

16. Single Minutes Exchange of Dies is a system for reducing the time it take to complete equipment changeovers. If this where the bottleneck is in your manufacturing process, then this is ideal. The essence of the SMED is to exchange as many changeover steps as possible to 'external', performed while the equipment is running, and to simplify and to streamline the remaining 'internal' steps.

True Story - The BI Team were asked to study the bottleneck machine in a production process: they observed a changeover, and detailed the improvements that could be made through re-sequencing the activities. Delighted with their efforts, they explained their ideas to the Manufacturing Manager, who promptly lost his temper, not at them, but at his engineers. 'They should have spotted this themselves', he said. True, and that's why independent BI Teams are called in.

17. JIT (Just-in-Time) – a methodology aimed at reducing flow times within production systems as well as response times from suppliers and to customers. Developed and largely perfected by Toyota Production Systems, it requires all managers and team members to be familiar with this way of working, and abide by the clear operating rules. Needs constant monitoring and adjusting if necessary,and can be quite dangerous if left unchecked.

True Story - A medium-sized engineering company had installed a new MRP system, mostly automated. When checking the forward planning, I noticed that there was a downward trend in both forecasted sales, and hence material requirements. As we were entering a peak trading season, I checked further: by manual calculations, these numbers were incorrect. So the company had to retrieve discarded machinery from the scrap-heap, re-employ employees they'd just made redundant, and ramp-up production to meet future demand. They were 'Just-in-Time'.

18. Margin Control – Nowadays, margin control is monitored by software programmes, which oversees sales, e-commerce, billing, accounting, manufacturing, warehouse and inventory. But I still have my trusty 'cost' and 'sell' buttons on my calculator, which automatically gives me the margin, which is the difference between the cost price and selling price of a product. That's why margin control throughout your process is critically important. Many businesses have inadequate controls in this area.

True Story: A large manufacturing company was building expensive and complex machines. I asked one of the Managers what the margin was after the unit had completed one of its build-stages. 'We don't know: we do transfer-pricing here'. That's a problem in the making, literally. If you're unsure of your value-add at each stage, then identifying at which stage you could reduce costs during difficult trading times is problematical.

19. Hoshin Kanri is at the heart of the strategy execution systems of the world's best-performing organizations. Organizations that adopt Hoshin Kanri consistently outperform their peers. Also known as Hoshin Planning, Policy Deployment, Goal Deployment and Priority Deployment, Hoshin Kanri helps organizations to consistently achieve their strategic goals and measure results. **Align and manage your business goals, projects and metrics** Digitally capture and cascade goals at all levels of your organization, encouraging two-way dialogue, feedback and clear connection to your strategy. But be very careful!

True Story – One large company invested a substantial amount of time and resources in a series of Hoshin Kanri events. They were excellent, except for the fact that the demand for their products was rapidly dwindling, so it was an expensive way to manage production volumes down.

20. Kaikaku: Lean production term which, in Japanese, means radical overhaul of an activity/process to eliminate all waste (muda) and create greater value. Also called Breakthrough Kaizen. Excellent Tool, seldom used, and the BI Leader needs to 'clear their desk' for a full week in order to focus on delivering and installing the improvements from the Workshop.

True Story - Having analysed the flow of work in a manufacturing cell, the BI Team decided to install a Single Piece Flow operation: we doubled productivity in the space of a few hours.

The Management Team didn't believe the results, so they took the place of the Line Operators: again, productivity doubled.

21. Capacity Release expands the production / process capacity whilst minimizing the cost of increasing that capacity. Usually occurs at the bottleneck position, then moving to the next bottleneck and so on: but can also involve the complete reconfiguration of the area, of work schedules, and the supply chain.

True Story: *One company had severe capacity constraints from a manufacturing process that was almost beyond belief: if I hadn't have spent hours observing the flow, I would not have believed the data. Progressively, over a few months, we scrapped the entire flow and started from scratch. New factory site, new layout, new procedures: everything improved. In BI terms, ensure that the Boss is aligned with the improvement   every step of the way.*

22. Waterfall Projects: Often thought of as the more 'traditional' methodology for managing a Project, with the Project approach being a favourite method for delivering business improvements. In essence, 'Waterfall' is a set of linear activities: a comparison to the 'Agile' approach is shown below, this example is for a BI software development:-

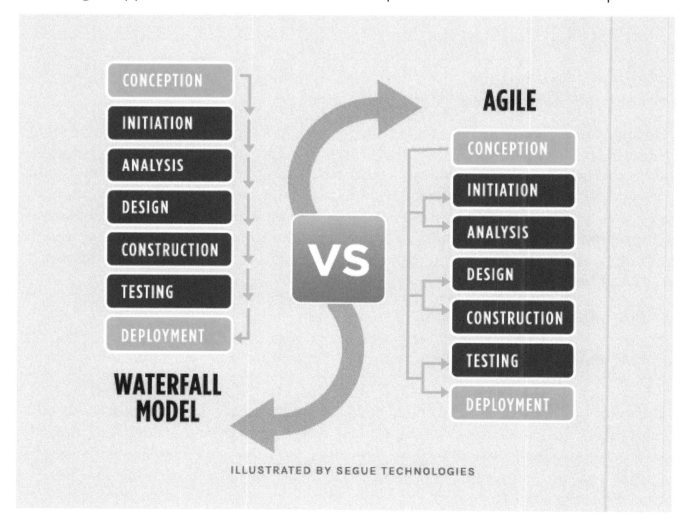

Fig 12: Waterfall vs. Agile Project Methodology   (Courtesy of Segue Engineering – comparison of two approaches to a software development project)

The benefits of a Waterfall approach are:-

1. The BI Team and their customers agree on what will be delivered early in the development life-cycle. This makes planning and designing more straightforward.

2. Progress is more easily measured, as the full scope of the work is known in advance.

3. Throughout the development effort, it's possible for various members of the team to be involved or to continue with other work, depending on the active phase of the BI project.

4. Except for reviews, approvals, status meetings, etc., *a customer presence is not strictly required after the requirements phase.*

5. Because design of new systems is completed early in the development life-cycle, this approach lends itself to projects where multiple components must be designed for integration with external systems: management operating systems (MOS) are a example.

Now look at some of the **issues** that (Segue Software) have encountered using a Waterfall approach:*One area which almost always falls short is the effectiveness of requirements. Gathering and documenting requirements in a way that is meaningful to a customer is often the most difficult part of software development,* In addition, the end product/service may not always be clear to customers. *Another potential drawback of Waterfall development is the possibility that the customer will be dissatisfied with their delivered software product. delivered until it's almost finished. By that time, changes can be difficult (and costly) to implement.* This is a typical list of the pros and cons of using a Waterfall approach for software development alone, or a combination of software within a BI context. Now let's look at the 'Agile' approach.

True Story - The Client had recruited an asset management software developer – just one. He worked studiously, in the same area as our BI Team: and, as the weeks went by, I wondered what, exactly, he was working on. Not being an IT expert, I thought it would be intellectually demanding. Not so: it was a report demonstrating that an algorithm could have financially out-performed the buy/sell decisions of all the traders employed by the Company. Goodbye traders! Sometimes the methodology you choose doesn't effect the business outcome: so keep the BI benefits in mind at all times.

23.   The Agile Methodology: 'Agile' is an iterative, team-based approach to development. Rather than creating tasks and schedules, all time is "time-boxed" into phases called "sprints." Each sprint has a defined duration (usually in weeks) with a running list of deliverables, planned at the start of the sprint. **Deliverables are prioritized by business value as determined by the customer.** If all planned work for the sprint cannot be completed, work is re-prioritized and the information is used for future sprint planning. As work is completed, it can be reviewed and evaluated by the project team and customer, through daily builds and end-of-sprint demonstrations. Agile relies on a **very high level of customer involvement** throughout the project, but especially during these reviews.

Three advantages of the Agile approach:-

1. The customer has frequent and early opportunities to see the work being delivered, and to make decisions and changes throughout the development project. 2. The customer gains a strong sense of ownership by working extensively and directly with the project team.

3. Development is often more user-focused, likely a result of more and frequent direction from the customer.

And there follows a list disadvantages, from a very high degree of customer involvement, a completely dedicated Team for the project, some items set for delivery not completed within the allotted time-frame, a lack of the full scope of the system is not considered in the initial architecture and design.

Whichever approach you decide upon, Segue have their own process. It's called the **Process Framework**[37], and it's a variation on the traditional Waterfall methodology, mixed with some elements of 'Agile'. And it acts as a lightweight **Business Cube**, trying to avoid project problems before they emerge. Eventually, it all comes down to *delivering a solid and maintainable product that satisfies our customer is what really counts.*

True Story - Sitting down with a banking software developer, after a few hours reviewing the current software coding, we realise that there are only two developers still employed by the company who are expert in this outdated code. Nobody had thought through the implications of this before letting these developers leave the company.

My argument: you need a structure and discipline to compel business owners and managers to consider all consequences of their decisions.

24. AI (Artificial Intelligence) makes it possible for machines to learn from experience, adjust to new inputs and perform human-like tasks. In a 2016 article from *Business Insider*, General Electric described what an ideal intelligent factory would look like. Their vision for the "Brilliant Factory[38]," as they called it, would start with automatic ordering based on detected customer need, and use 3D printing technologies to design, prototype, and test a new part in hours rather than days or weeks. Streamlining production would be next, with highly intelligent robots bearing a majority of the assembly workload. These stages would be continuously monitored by artificial intelligence (AI) technologies to detect abnormalities or faults, and eliminate downtime in the process. Current artificial intelligence opportunities allows manufacturing to become smarter, with a focus on research and development, procurement, and assembly line processes.

True Story - An automated production line suddenly stopped working in mid-cycle: I know because I was there. After several days, we realised that the software programme controlling that key machine had been repeatedly modified, and nobody knew what the original specification was, or what modifications had been made. So our BI assignment was in severe trouble.

There was maintenance access to the machine located on the underside: the engineer crawled into the space and completed checks on key components. I did likewise and simply replaced the automated activity with my human hands. Nobody thought it would work, but it did: so after demonstrating how to do this, we re-trained the crew to work inside the machine. Fortunately, there were no health and safety concerns present. And we were able to maintain the same machine/production line speed as before. Remember to keep your BIs simple!

25. RFID (Radio Frequency Identification) automatically identifies and tracks tags attached to objects. An RFID tag consists of a tiny radio transponder; a radio receiver and transmitter. When triggered by an electromagnetic interrogation pulse from a nearby RFID reader device, the tag transmits digital data, usually an identifying inventory number, back to the reader. This number can be used to inventory goods. RFID has proved invaluable throughout all types of warehouses anywhere in the world. It's a hidden and often forgotten BI which has delivered significant savings and benefits.

26. RTLS (Real Time Location Systems) are used to automatically identify and track the location of objects or people in real time, usually within a building or other contained area. Wireless **RTLS** tags are attached to objects or worn by people, and in most **RTLS**, fixed reference points receive wireless signals from tags to determine their location.

True Story - The case of the missing chickens. For years, birds were vanishing whilst in transit to processing plants. No RTLS or RFID for them: so we tried the old-fashioned approach of observing many journeys. Eventually the facts emerged: some vehicles had hidden compartments beneath the floor, and a few birds just disappeared every time. But never enough on one trip to arouse anybody's suspicions. After a few years, the numbers of missing chickens were very substantial.

27. KPIs (Key Performance Indicators) / Scorecard – 'Show me the reward system, and I'll show you people's behaviour'. So KPIs are absolutely vital, and their alignment with the business goals are also critical . A Scorecard brings all the information together in one overall performance presentation that can be reviewed on a weekly basis. So data gathered by minute or event translates into hourly reporting, which can be by shift, per day, then weekly into monthly reports. And the reported numbers can be then trended and compared – and used to create reliable forecasts for sales , marketing, production, logistics etc.

True Story: A large food processing plant incentivized its managers by matching production volumes to bonus payments. So volumes surged, and so did bonuses, and so did processed waste. By careful what you incentivize your people for.

28. Margins – In section 18, we covered Margin Control. This is the only subject that is discussed twice under the Tools heading. That's how important it is. So without repeating the previous section, the accurate and timely reporting of margins on each transaction is vital, and should be an integral part of any business's 'KPIs/ Scorecard'.

29. Cash Control – Cash is King, or a business account debit card with a lot of credit is now king. Cash control is an important part of business as it is required for proper cash management, monitoring and recording of cash flow and analyzing cash balance. Cash is the most important liquid asset of the business. A business concern cannot prosper and survive without proper control over cash. In accounting, cash includes coins, currency, deposited negotiable instruments such as cheques, bank drafts, and money orders, amounts in checking and savings accounts and demand certificates of deposit. Use cash to leverage a purchasing advantage. And always ensure you have a sum of cash available for business contingencies.

That's the 29 business improvement tools that I would look at first: there are dozens of others (e.g. there are about 44 different software programming methodologies[39] alone). **But never fall in love with the tools without understanding each one: and never fall in love with the tools when you should be in love with the benefits of business improvements.**

The Boss decides which 'Drivers' require business improvement. Now there'll be a Senior Management Team proposing various improvements that should be considered, but there needs to be only one decision-maker: and that person is the Boss (No.1 Doll). So when BI Leaders refer to involving the Senior Management Team to gain their support, 'support' is often all that you'll get. What is required is impetus, that push to get the BI started and seen through to a delivering the promised results. Out of the 35 projects that I've been involved with, only one has been a complete failure. In that case, the VCs had recruited a seasoned Top Manager to lead their recently-purchased acquisition, and he lived in the South of France: the business was based in Essex. So where do you think he spent most of his time? Impossible for the BI Leader and Team to sustain any improvements with 'remote' support. There has to be a clear and direct line of communication between the BI Leader and the Boss with the Business Drivers on the firm Agenda. Not just the current Driver and chosen Improvement, but all of the Drivers. The fact is that business circumstances constantly change: if these changes impact your BI, find out before the event. Almost every one of these meetings I've attended in my 35 years has focused on the BI update only: you have to broaden the topic to include the whole business. This helps with aligning the BI with all other areas of the business: and this becomes increasingly important over time.

So the BI Meeting has an agenda, and the Boss and Senior Management Team have to attend. It's not just about an update: it's also about positioning the BI within the whole business. Is it still meeting the businesses' requirements? Is there a danger of Scope Creep? Has the requirement evaporated?

True Story - Three days into a BI assignment, the client company is taken over: the BI Leaders are summoned to a meeting with the new Top Boss. We're authorized to continue the Improvement, much to our surprise! Always maintain clear lines of communication with the Top Boss, no matter what the possible outcomes.

Business Improvement Opportunities: there'll probably be a long list. Apply the logic of Sherlock Holmes: **'If the data proves a hypothesis wrong in favour of a seemingly improbable result, admit that the data proved you wrong. Be open'.**

True Story - A daily review at 8.00am every morning briefed one of the senior managers on the performance of his business unit. Unfortunately, on one of the mornings, the numbers presented were clearly wrong. 'Can't we trust the numbers any more?', he asked. There was complete silence from all attendees. Can you trust your numbers?

Top of any lists would be cash-flow, bottlenecks, sales drop and margin erosion: so there's a full spectrum of contenders. It's at this point the Business Cube kicks in. Taking the chosen BI, start on the first Layer, first Block and think through the questions that need to be asked. And when you don't ask those questions, this is what can happen....

True Story - Just starting a new BI assignment: then we discovered that the final legal contract and agreement between ourselves and the Client had doubled our workload by including a separate company that few people had even known about.

Lack of thinking, lack of using the Cube before the BI Team had even begun work, and a slapdash approach to running any business. Which is one powerful reason why a Cube approach brings clarity and discipline to what can be an unstructured event.

The Cube has three core elements: Resources, Standards and Management Systems. And each of these are split into three elements themselves. There is nothing intellectual or sophisticated about this approach. It is based on my 35 years of BI experience on the 'front-line'. Unlike my contemporaries, I never had any desire to move up the 'promotion ladder', becoming a senior executive or Director, with a decreasing level of direct contact with BI Teams and Clients. So my 35 years is 'up close and personal', as the Americans would say: the incentive to succeed and avoid disastrous project outcomes has always been a key driver for me. Job preservation has a lot to be said for it!

Dropping a stranger into a failing business is acceptable, providing you're not the stranger. So when your Boss says 'go fix this business', a structured approach is essential. That usually involves a copy of the latest set of accounts, internal reports and a management organization chart. Useful, but not the information that will guide your thinking on the way forward. If you take the first of the three Layers, People, then start there, with the No.1 Boss. And be careful.....

True Story* -* The Boss of a large food processing company decided to show me their operations across the road. We walked into the loading dock, then he stopped and looked around: 'Oh, wrong factory', he said: and it was another company's loading dock. Perhaps he was part of the problem, not the solution.

Once you've engaged with the Boss and the Senior Team, ask to be introduced to the Supervisors. This may seem illogical, because you should be meeting the middle managers next. From my experience, there are only two levels of management that are critical for a successful BI initiative: the Boss and the Supervisory level; it's all to do with the Russian Doll, and the way influence and authority of the No. 1 Doll permeates throughout the business. And I will quote Alastair Mant's[40] book 'Leaders We Deserve' (1983), page 24:-

The boys at the top *: not necessarily very clever or very responsible but at least capable safe enough to think about alternatives; rather isolated from the consumers; ageing now so that ternary considerations are beginning to bear in from other existences.*
The people at the bottom *of the organizations, producers and consumers (who may be married to each other), many of whom care about the standards, quality and the purpose of things (but maybe not obviously at work) and most of whom are resigned to staying at, or near, the bottom.*
The risers in the middle, *focused on competition and movement rather than the verities of life, and perpetually threatened by the possibility of 1. and 3. talking to each other. The risers are at an age when binary considerations tend to crowd out morals; a few of them are really dangerous. [particularly the sub-clinical psychopaths] Author's note. Never a truer word written!*

The Parts and Process Layer has received the most BI attention for many years. Focusing on cost reduction, this emphasis has tended to exclude the other Layers, which has not helped the growth and development of many businesses.

True Story* -* We needed a Sales and Marketing perspective on a Process Improvement Project we were delivering for a UK company. Having contacted the Marketing Director's office, we were told that the earliest appointment date for a meeting was in 3 month's time. The meeting never took place.

And that's the problem with organization charts and Departments. Very few senior managers, and sometimes the Boss, understand that their products and/or services are a complete, uninterrupted flow of work and, hopefully, value add for all their stakeholders. So why would the Marketing Director's input be required for a process improvement project?

True Story* -* The 7 companies listed in this 'Process Excellence' article are Ford, Bell Labs., Motorola, GE, Dell, Toyota and Amazon. Most of these are household names: and they have all fared very differently in the business world. Some are a shadow of their former selves (Motorola, Nokia Bell Labs. and GE): some are weathering the COVID -19 pandemic (Ford, Toyota, Dell Technologies) as best they can, and one is just surging ahead (Amazon). Yet they were all lauded for process excellence in 2014.

So why is Amazon surging ahead? Apart from the 'COVID-19' impact, which has boosted on-line sales and services in 2020, there have been hundreds of articles and books on the reasons for Amazon's success. To my mind, there are just two key factors: Jeff Bezos and the delivery of his 'Big Picture' view of Amazon. So it's the influence of the Boss, and their complete understanding of the vision to grow both company sales and margins. In other words, the No.1 Doll and his Business Cube.

Too simplistic: not complicated enough for a business textbook? I've witnessed this combination of individual determination with a clear vision and execution in 4 of my 35 assignments that I've worked with.

5. USING THE CUBE[41]

Logical Levels Model

- Cube
- The Boss: No.1
- Purpose
- Identity
- Senior Management No.2
- Layers
- Beliefs and Values
- Middle Management No.3
- Capability
- Blocks
- Behaviour
- Supervisory No.4
- Tools
- Environment
- Workforce No.5
- The Business Cube
- The Russian Dolls

The Implementation Model

The Logical Levels model *was created by Robert Dilts, building on the work of Gregory Bateson. This model is widely used in personal development and business coaching. You can use it both as a diagnostic to help clients consider where the business is currently and also as a planning tool to elicit rich data to support the development of mission and vision.* ***It can also be useful when coaching leaders who are planning for change.*** (Business Coaching & Mentoring For Dummies, 2nd Edition, Marie Taylor, Steve Crabb).

A brief explanation of the 6 stages shown in the Logical Levels Model (LLM):-

Environment

This refers to everything outside of yourself and is the state of the external context in which people are living and acting - where and when our actions are taking place.

Behaviour

This relates to the specific steps taken in order to respond to the environment and reach a desired outcome. They involve what must be done and accomplished.

Capabilities

This refers to the mental maps, plans, strategies, skills and capabilities by which groups or individuals select and direct the steps they take within their environment. They direct how steps are generated, selected and monitored.

Beliefs and Values

These provide the drivers that support or inhibit particular capabilities and behaviours. They relate to why a particular path is taken and to the deeper drivers of people's actions.

Identity

These factors are a function of who a person or group perceives themselves to be. This level has to do with the unique, distinguishing characteristics that define an individual, group or organisation.

Purpose

This relates to people's experience of contributing to the larger system of which they are a part. These factors involve for whom or for what a particular step or path has been taken.

I've always enjoyed using the Logical Levels Model - so why doesn't it appear in my list of 29 Tools? Two reasons: firstly, it can be dangerous to use with the Boss and Senior Management if you're not fully trained and qualified. And secondly, it struggles to be integrated with other BITs. So it's a stand-alone Tool, like a warm-up act in a Business Improvement cabaret show. You can switch the audience 'on' with it, but then have to lead them somewhere else for the main event.

So the LLM is unique: I'm unable to think of any other Tool that can explain the opportunities for personal improvement better than this. If you include the Russian Dolls in the Model, then you can align the Levels that are most applicable to each Doll. From my experience, Workforce members will be focused on 4 levels Beliefs and Values, Capabilities, Behaviour and Environment. Or their Beliefs about the business, their Values within the business, their skills and training, what they do and where they do it.

True Story: One production line was housed beneath a massive skylight in the roof - excellent for lighting purposes, but very hot in the summer months. So we arranged for a water cooler to be installed in their working area, instead of taking a 10 minute walk to the cafeteria. Workforce delighted, productivity rises, and a 'win-win' situation. Nobody had thought of this before.

In LLM terms, we changed our behaviour (fitted a water cooler) to improve our environment (drink a cup of water when needed) to improve performance. We had the capability to do this (could source a plumber and equipment supplier) and our belief was that some employees were sometimes thirsty. The simple value: the employee's welfare matters. Think througbh the implications for supervisors and managers - they make decisions that directly or indirectly impact the performance of your business. And the business improvements that you need to be implement.

But the fundamental flaw to delivering successful business improvements still remained - sustainability, or the lack of it.

True Story: We once went 'head-to-head' with a rival productivity performance consultancy. Two separate BIs were started at the same time to discover which approach had more 'stickability'. Our approach won - it was never clear exactly what the winning criteria was, but we did think about 'which differences made the difference', and that was how 'Cube' thinking originated.

From there, over many years, the Cube was refined, eventually linking up with both the LLM and the Russian Dolls. At that point, we were nearing an end-point - a point where you're able to confidently sit down with the Boss and explain, with the use of a single side of A4 paper, exactly how the Business Improvement will be delivered.

Using the Cube - with the Boss - Looking at '**Using the Cube'** , the Boss is fully aligned with both Purpose and Identity - only once have I found a Boss who was not, and the recommendation was redundancy. What the Boss will not be aligned with is what needs to be done by him or her. Defining the BI goals, setting the time-frame, chairing the Opening meeting and weekly review meetings, and independently monitoring the BI results is a brief overview. More importantly, the Boss (No.1) sets the behaviour standards for the senior management team (No.2), and they will set those standards for their middle managers (No.3): and so on, until the very last sub-contractor is engaged.

At any time, the Cube, Layers and Blocks can be explained: how they can be aware of the whole business and any of the details at any time. Because the Cube provides **transparency**: what's called 'shining a light' in dark performance places. And try to steer clear of discussing the Tools - in many cases, the Boss has heard about the latest management fad which may, or may not, be the most applicable Tool for improving the business. And all of this can be done from a single sheet of paper.

Using the Cube - with Senior Management - It appears that senior and middle managers are grouped together in '**Using the Cube**': in fact, they also cover 'Identity', 'Beliefs and Values' and 'Capabilities', the same levels in the LLM. In current management terminology, these are the occupiers of the 'C' Suite: after the Boss, they are the next group that are critically important for your BI. And they are all working off the BI script - simply emphasise different aspects that apply to their respective areas.

True Story: The Boss had already been 'positioned' some two month's earlier for an assignment that had made little progress. So we convened a business development workshop with the senior management team that addressed a long-standing issue in their group of companies - margin control. Using the same format as in '**Using the Cube'**, we brought the two Russian Dolls into one project.

Using the Cube - with Middle Management - Often the Doll that provides the most problems for Business Improvements. I think this is where a de-layering of management levels is often useful. They love meetings, and it can be difficult identifying their value-add to the business. But it's necessary to work with people at all levels, so ensure they're always involved with a defined purpose.

Using the Cube - with Supervisors - After Dolls 1 and 2, Doll No.4 is the most important for your BI success. They supervise the Workforce, and have a direct impact on behaviour and performance. They can either support, remain ambivalent or denigrate your BI - their support is critical to the success of your BI.

Using the Cube - with the Workforce - Whether they are unionised, non-unionised, or just sub-contractors, they are the essential to success. When it's difficult to be aligned with everybody, you may have to make some tough decisions.

True Story: Walking into the factory canteen, I was warmly welcomed by one of the site's leading trade union representatives, who led the key group of skilled workers on site. Seated behind him were the representatives of the largest group of unskilled workers on site: they were looking very unhappy. Moral of the story: best to align with the key workers every time.

Using the Cube - you need some Rules

To get the best out of the **Business Cube**, there are only three Rules:-

1. There's only *one Cube for any Business Unit*. That Unit may be the whole company, a division of the company, or a discrete entity within a business. Preferably, it's the whole business.

2. There are always three Layers and twenty seven Blocks in any Business Cube: they run sequentially, and never change.

3. Wherever you think your Improvement lies within the Cube, always start thinking at Block 1, working progressively through to Block 27. Please don't skip a Block or two. Make a note of all the factors that could impact your Improvement, and all the business elements that could be impacted by your Improvement.

Start filling out each Block, sequentially...work towards the Blocks that offer benefits...**mention the FMEA aspect of the Cube** - 'Failure Mode Effects (or Evaluation) Analysis'[42] for BI.....Take one day to prepare the Cube with your Team, preferably off-site. This is not brainstorming[43], nor creative thinking[44], or mind-mapping[45], or a check-list[46], Six Thinking Hats[47], Lateral thinking[48], the Ishikawa Tree[49] (Fishbone), SWOT analysis[50], 'stair-step'[51] critical thinking model, flexible thinking[52], structured thinking[53] (Pyramid Principle) etc.

Place all these Tools inside the Cube, if you want to - the **Cube represents structured thinking** for those who haven't the project time to fire-fight problems that could have been foreseen. So use the Cube to channel your thinking towards the BI goals. Otherwise you can have a scatological approach - the 'shotgun' approach that allows you to work gradually towards the BI outcomes at a more leisurely pace.

The Cube evolved from managing **business improvements when under pressure** - pressure from VCs., pressure from customers, stakeholders, etc. When businesses are going into bankruptcy, when there's a need to achieve results now. So the **Cube + Russian Dolls + LLM** are powerful when you absolutely have to achieve the Business Improvement now......when every hour counts. If you're business is coasting along, margins are good, sales are trending upwards, costs are under control, then use some other tool if you want to: or do nothing!

6. LET'S GET STARTED - NOW!

Let's understand how a traditional Business Improvement assignment is started compared with a Cube-based approach:-

Project	Traditional BI Project Approach	Business Cube Approach
Week 0	Project plan, Scoping document, Payback schedule	Cube Development - Blocks 1 - 27
Week 1	Pre-presentation Opening Meeting Kick-off Meeting Detailed work plan	Project plan, Scoping schedule Pre-presentation Opening Meeting Kick-off Meeting Cube update, detailed work plan

Both of these Approaches should be supported by an initial Business Analysis that identifies areas and opportunities for improvement. But not always: sometimes the Analysis is superficial or focused on one particular aspect of the business. It is often geared towards 'selling' a Business Improvement rather than information gathering to support a BI - and the information can be flawed. Starting afresh with a one-day 'Cube' Analysis will allow the BI Leader and Team to understand exactly what data they need to gather to deliver an effective BI. With the traditional Approach, this normally happen during the first two project weeks - a kind of 'learn-as-you-go' experience after the Project plan has been prepared and presented. That Plan will incorporate the Business Analysis information and the wisdom of the BI Leader - which can be adequate, providing the Analysis information is sound and the BI Leader is experienced. Not always the case.

The practicalities of conducting a one-day 'Cube' Analysis are simple. There are 27 Blocks, all of which need to be completed sequentially, and there are 8 hours in an average working day. So 27 x 15 minutes per Block = 6.75 hours on the Cube. Which allows 45 minutes for lunch, with two 15 minutes tea breaks. That allows enough time to define the data and information requirements for the BI, and improve the quality of the required Plan. There are two benefits here: firstly, better preparation before the Opening Meeting with the Boss, and secondly, a more critical assessment of what is really needed to deliver the BI benefits. A kind of 'Failure Mode Effects (or Evaluation) Analysis' (FMEA) of the Business Improvement before actually starting the assignment. This reduces the amount of rework needed to adjust the Plan after the assignment has started - it is essentially a more professional way of working.

During the Thursday afternoon of each working week, when the BI Weekly Meeting is refining the Plan for the coming week, return to the Cube output from Week 0 and check that nothing has been overlooked.

True Story: Reviewing the progress of a BI project, we noticed a single sentence comment at the foot of one document. Believing that this had been forgotten by the Team, we checked back through our notes to discover that it had been actioned. Traceability is a key ingredient for any project, and the Cube allows you to see where **structured business thinking** originates, and to track it through to present day.

Whether your business is large, medium-sized or small, makes no difference to the Cube process: it's applicable for any type of business, from manufacturing to software development, and any type of 'project-planning' methodology you're currently using.

Let's take one example. You're the Leader for a software development assignment, and there's an installation deadline your Boss is determined to keep. So a 'project tracker' is being used to monitor progress, and everything seems to be 'on-track'. Or is it? In the traditional BI Approach, the Leader would check the accuracy of progress reporting: some 'deep dives' into the details of the work, asking '5 - Whys' to understand the programming logic. The Cube Approach encourages this as well - then moves the discussion about project execution further forward. Before the project starts, the Cube Analysis could reveal the fact that all programmers and software developers have different benchmarks for measuring progress - more of a personal preference than a technical assessment. So some progress steps could be over-estimated, and some under-estimated: and the impact of that depends on their status along the critical path. This reality-check can be addressed before the project starts: if individuals in your Team exaggerate their progress within the project, then there will be consequences. If they understate their progress, then the consequences will be less: so accurate reporting is a pre-requisite for successful project completion. And this reality has to be clearly understood from the start.

True Story: It's **Friday, 20th April, 2018, at 4pm.**, and the **TSB**[54] **(Trustee Savings Bank) begins a long-planned IT upgrade,** transferring the records and accounts of its 5.2 million customers from a system operated by its former owner, Lloyds Banking Group, to one designed by its current owner, the Spanish Banco Sabadell[55]. TSB warns customers that some services, such as on-line banking and money transfers, will not be available until 6pm on Sunday 22 April.

Its now **Monday 23rd April,** 2018, and the **TSB plays down the "access issues"**, saying it is experiencing intermittent problems with its internet banking and mobile app. affecting a limited number of customers. However, customers in increasing numbers make their feelings known on Twitter, complaining that they cannot access their accounts. TSB's parent company, Sabadell, makes an embarrassing gaffe by publishing a **statement on its website saying it has "successfully completed the TSB technology migration".**

Its now **Tuesday 24 April:** The botched IT upgrade becomes a full-blown crisis as up to 1.9 million of TSB's online and mobile customers remain locked out of their accounts.

Its now **Monday 30 April: The chaos enters a second week**, with some TSB customers still unable to access accounts or make payments. MPs on the Treasury committee announce that they have called Dr. Pester (CEO TSB Group) – along with the bank's chair, Richard Meddings, and a representative from Spanish parent group Sabadell – to give evidence on the IT meltdown. **Part of this evidence is as follows:-**

Q181 Stephen Hammond (MP): Point 3 of the same section of your letter says that one of your objectives is to ensure that **TSB has a coherent plan for recovery of services.**

Andrew Bailey (Chief Executive Officer & Director, Financial Conduct Authority): Yes.

Q182 Stephen Hammond: Where are we in the time-line on having a coherent plan for recovery of services?

John Sutherland (MP): What it has at the moment is a **forward plan**. It is a **rolling fortnight forward plan** for fixing faults that have been identified in the IT. **We have not yet seen an overall plan** that says, "Having done these things, we expect to be at the service level that we were pre-migration". I am not saying it does not have it but we have not seen it yet.

Q183 Stephen Hammond: You would expect to see that in the near future. Would you not have expected that to be provided for you already?

Andrew Bailey: One of the things that came up in the last hearing is that one of the reasons it had to bring IBM in pretty quickly was that it *exactly did not have that plan.* One of the things that IBM has been most focused on is *putting that plan together*. To be fair to IBM, it was a cold start for IBM, so it had to get its arms around it.

Charlie Elphicke: Turning back to that letter then, you say first-time log-in success rates are at normal levels of over 92% for the mobile app and over 97% for the website. Presumably those are average figures.

Dr Pester (CEO TSB): Yes, those are taken all through the day of how many people attempt to log on and are successful first time, through the day.

Q290 Charlie Elphicke: Andrew Bailey says you have this *habit of quoting average figures and he warns you to be careful about doing that,* but here you are just yesterday. This letter was sent yesterday, so it was not sent ages ago. That "this was a long time ago" excuse does not work. You sent this to the Committee yesterday. Can you understand why we are quite cross that you seem to present information in a way that the average person would find misleading?

Wednesday 2 May 2018

Pester appears at the Treasury committee alongside Meddings and Sabadell's Miguel Montes. Nicky Morgan, the committee's chair, accuses Pester of being **"extraordinarily complacent"** after he says the IT upgrade had mostly run smoothly. Meddings says Pester will give up a £2m bonus associated with the IT migration but he could still receive up to £1.3m in other bonuses for 2018, on top of a further £1.3m in basic pay, benefits and pension contributions.

By the 27th of July 2018: the IT issues had **cost the TSB £176.4m.** The IT and data migration issues suffered earlier in the year have pushed the bank into a loss, its half-year results reveal.

Tuesday 4th September 2018: TSB boss Paul Pester will leave the troubled bank with a payout of nearly £1.7 million despite standing down in the wake of a botched IT switch and a string of ongoing technology failures. The lender confirmed Mr Pester, who has been placed on gardening leave, will get £1.2 million in severance pay and a "historical" bonus of around £480,000 that is due from before TSB's takeover by Sabadell in 2015.

The reason for re-printing these questions and answers by the Parliamentary Select Committee, and focusing on the TSB software upgrade at length, is that it encapsulates most of the common flaws in current Business Improvement deliveries:-

1.   Management issues within TSB - the calibre of management at a senior level to oversee an IT project to upgrade software systems.
2.   Lack of senior management focus on the IT project management, delivery and customer service.
3.   Ineffective project planning.
4.   Ineffective reporting and communicating between the IT upgrade Team, TSB management, customers and even the UK Parliament.

Yet the underlying failure is well-disguised. At the end of each project week, the different sub-Teams updated progress against their project plans. Using a common 'Green','Orange' and 'Red' signal system that tells everybody whether the Team are 'on-schedule', 'lagging' or 'off-schedule' respectively, some Teams **got into the habit of over-stating their current performance.** In isolation, this could have been rectified, or an effort made to catch-up with the overall Plan, or perhaps delay the 'Go Live' for the system's upgrade. That didn't happen: instead, Senior Management authorized the go-ahead without realizing that the project was off-schedule. Failure was the inevitable outcome. Interestingly enough, the same casual approach that Dr. Pester adopted with the Parliamentary Committee was present during the project delivery - putting 'creative' spin on the actual performance numbers. Which links the 'Cube' with the Russian Dolls - and if you factor in the Logical Levels Model, then the 'Beliefs' (and probably 'Values') were adrift as well.

And similar lessons could be learned from the UK Train Timetable upgrade of June 2108, or the London Crossrail Project of 2009 with no light at the end of the tunnel, or the Libra Software System for Magistrates. Primary reason for these failures was a lack of **structured, in-depth thinking** before the project started, coupled with ineffective management during the project life-cycle.

Thinking about the **Business Cube**, what would you have done differently as the BI Leader, or as the Boss? What will you do differently when you receive project progress reports early on Monday morning? Firstly, you need to be receiving these reports on Thursday afternoon, not Monday morning: so you need to change the reporting timetable. Look at the Cube and work out how many Blocks are impacted: don't be concerned with individuals, or Teams, or organization charts; that will come later. **So understand the Big Picture first**: then work through the Layers, and then understand the detail inside the Blocks. Thinking from **'Big to Detail'** is almost a lost skill for many Senior Managers - they sometimes live in a world of packaged and sanitized reports, in an environment of just **'running the numbers'**, like managing a business on autopilot. Which is exactly how Amazon.com is not run. The level of management attention from Big Picture to individual Customer Experience is compulsive: and that's driven by the Boss, Jeff Bezos. Again, there's a link between Cube thinking and the Russian Dolls: when you combine **'Big to Detail'** with a highly focused Boss, then the business, or business improvement, will succeed dramatically.

From the extraordinarily successful to the Grenfell Tower Fire[56] of 14th June 2017. A fire broke out in the 24-storey Grenfell Tower block of flats in North Kensington, West London, at 00:54 BST; it caused 72 deaths, including those of two victims who later died in hospital. More than 70 others were injured and 223 people escaped. This improvement project for the Grenfell Tower is now the subject of a major Public Inquiry. Although the full findings are yet to be published, it is clear from the evidence so far that:-

1.   There was a calamitous failure to plan and execute an upgrade to the exterior of the building.
2.   That failure was endemic at every level, from project management to architects to sub-contractors.

And there are other underlying reasons that have emerged. The then head of the London Fire Brigade (LFB), when asked by the Inquiry Chairman what she would have done differently in hindsight, told the public inquiry she would not have done anything differently, a remark that the Inquiry chairman said showed "remarkable insensitivity". It also shows a remarkable resistance to learning from experience or evidence. When the Boss resists change, even after catastrophe, then you need to examine the criteria for recruitment and selection at the top level.

Take poor leadership and management of Rescue Services, couple it with indifferent project management and a lack of supervision, then you have a recipe for disaster. And this was predicted by one of the co-leaders of the Grenfell Action Group that had said, some eight months before the tragedy, that due to the neglect of their landlord the block could be catastrophically destroyed by fire.

He was right.

A Cube approach would have identified several inherent defects in the planned upgrade of the Tower - an understanding of the Russian Dolls would have flagged the lack of management throughout the Project. I wonder what the outcome of the high-speed train line project[57] (HS2) will be?

Have I frightened you into adopting a more structured thinking approach to business improvements before even starting the assignment? I hope so: and here are a few *True Stories* to reinforce your fear.

True Stories: The BI Team arrived in the Control Room of a Liquified Natural Gas Plant: there was a noticeably subdued atmosphere in the room, and we eventually found out why. Overnight, there had been a large gas leak from one of the main pipelines supplying the offshore gas into the Plant: it was in one of the areas where the Team had been denied access, and a later inspection of the main pipe showed what had happened. The pipe had ruptured at it's weakest point, and the only good news was that there was a gentle offshore breeze blowing at the time. None of the detectors had picked up the leak immediately, and the pipe had not had any maintenance for 3 years. *The message: effective maintenance is not an option! It's a necessity, unless you want to injure yourself or your team members.*

THREE WORKING EXAMPLES:

November 3rd 2019 by Dr. Wendy Tietz, CPA, CMA, CSCA, CGMA, Copyright 2019 Wendy M. Tietz, LLC wtietz@kent.edu The University of British Columbia - Accounting in the Headlines - **Case Study**

At Cleveland Hopkins International Airport in north eastern Ohio, a vending machine that dispenses socks was recently installed. Located in the 'C' concourse, the Stance™ sock vending machine offers a variety of what Stance refers to as "uncommon" socks. The designs on the socks in the Cleveland airport vending machine include Cleveland Browns, Cleveland Indians, patriotic flag designs, Hawaiian tropical flowers, and others. The machine is stocked with an assortment of socks. The airport traveller inserts a credit card, makes a sock selection in the keypad, and the socks are dispensed to the purchaser. Stance sells its socks through retailers, at its own stores, via vending machines, and through monthly subscriptions.

Current sales of socks from the vending machine are just covering the operating costs. **Outline a business improvement plan (BIP) to increase sales and reduce operating costs.**

You've decided to use the Cube approach. Identify the Blocks and Tools that are involved in, and may be impacted by, delivering a successful business outcome - which is to increase sales, reduce costs, and improve profits. Using the Cube, identify the Blocks that are most impacted - then list the Tools and actions that need to be taken to deliver the BI. (e.g. Increase Sales - Marketing plan, sales promotions, new site locations for Stance products. Use whatever Tool works for your Team: perhaps a 'Fishbone' analysis, remembering to place it within the 'Cube' rules - this reduces the chances of omitting a critical action.

True Story: Precious Metal Refiner and Processor

The Director of Operations for a medium-sized processing plant decided to improve security and efficiency in his area by installing a number of sea containers converted into compartmented process units. More than 50% of the workforce were located in these containers. There were a few operating problems, not least that the local Health and Safety Inspectors visited the site and immediately closed the premises, locking the gates until further notice. The entire operation of 360 people moved location over the weekend, and restarted work at 8.00am next Monday morning, some 6 miles from the original site.

And to confirm those facts, I've attached a photograph of the inside of one of the containers. The flow of work was from one end of the container to the other, work being transported in white buckets. The ergonomics were non-existent, and, when all team members were at their work-stations, movement through the container work-stations was difficult. There were no 'Fire Exits' as such, but the problem that closed the premises was the fact that all the electrical wiring was jury-rigged: they had connected all the containers to the electrical supply with just regular plugs and extension leads. The bottom photograph was the processing area in the new factory.

Top, the sea container layout: **Bottom,** the new layout.

Using the Cube approach, identify which Blocks form the core of the business improvement, and which Blocks are impacted by them. Then list the tools required to deliver the BI, and align your Russian Dolls accordingly.

Patisserie Valerie[58]:

In late 2018, it became apparent that the accounts produced by this company were fake and had been heavily manipulated with fraudulent and significant irregularities. The company declared, through an internal report, that this fraud had been detected. The company was extremely short of capital. What I find amazing is that even some of the management team were unaware of what was occurring behind their backs until of course their bank accounts had been frozen. At the last company presentation [8], the company stated how £28 million as net cash was sitting on its balance sheet. This was far from the truth, as was discovered in October. Instead of £28 million of cash, the company was in £10 million of debt. That difference between the numbers by £38 million wasn't a silly mistake, but rather it was clear manipulation. The company's operations were extremely dubious. Cheques were being paid that bounced and suppliers and landlords were being paid as late as possible before legal action was taken. Flour, butter and cream alongside shop fittings, refrigeration equipment, software/technology and even land is required to operate bakeries; so, when annoyed suppliers cut off their supply, the business suffers terrible downside effects. Having lost patience, suppliers even turned up at Patisserie Valerie's offices in Birmingham with baseball bats, demanding payment. There was an elaborate operation occurring to make the company seem more profitable than it actually was. **I think this reflects the human tendency to believe and see what one wants to – wilful thinking.**

Using the Cube approach, what would your Business Improvement Plan look like? How would you align the future Russian Dolls?

If you have managed to complete the first Case Study, then well done! If you managed to complete the second, then I'm impressed. And if you completed the third one, then you should have been doing my old job! These examples are real: they actually happened, because in two of the cases I was there. Two out of the three have issues with the Russian Dolls at a Senior Management Level, and two lack the structured thinking that should have been done to prevent significant operating problems. And to help you along the path of understanding, I've taken the second example and started a Block-by-Block approach by using the Cube. Just turn back to the previous page and re-read about the Precious Metal Refiner. Then remind yourself about the Cube.

If we can agree that the Business Improvement lies in the Parts & Process Layer, in Blocks 13 to 18, which involves Control and Report / Review, Safety / Quality, Quantity and Time, particularly the Safety and Quality elements of 'Parts / Process Standards'. Now you need to measure the scale of the issue: you can use the Safety Officer's approach when he inspected the premises, which involved 'just one look' and then hand over eyes, or you can compare with the State Statutory requirements for electrical fittings in factory premises. Let's agree that the premises failed the inspection.

The Cube Rules state that you move to Block 1 to start thinking through the Business Improvement: Block 1 is **'People - Forecast/Plan - Safety/Quality'** - so any improvements will definitely involve this Block. Here's a list of potential improvement Tools and Actions.

1. Get a copy of the latest Building / Electrical Statutory regulations - read it.
2. Get a copy of the latest Fire Regulations for commercial premises - read that as well.
3. Compare the Inspector's Report with your premises and the Regulatory requirements.

Q1. Could the current factory layout ever meet **forecast or planned** requirements on **Health and Safety criteria** for any number of **People?** In this case, the answer was 'No'.

Action: Search for suitable premises to transfer processing operations.

Time: **Now** - so in **LLM terms**, you know it's some**(where)** else, you know it's a factory transfer **(what)**, you know your Team have the **ability** to locate another site quickly, and you **believe** this is the best and right course of action for the business.

In **Russian Doll terms**, the Boss has just had his factory closed, so he needs to fix this problem now. The Senior Management Team have really screwed up, so they are automatically aligned with the Boss, and the Middle Managers are busy looking for a new site. Supervisors need to focus on retaining the employees on the payroll and think about a new site when time allows.

You will have realised that there are dozens of points to be made in Block 1 alone: so get an A0 pad of flip-chart paper and easel, and start writing down these points in black marker pen: label the first sheet 'Block 1' in the top-left hand corner, and mark all items with a red marker for 'Most Immediate' items, then orange for the next level etc.: this prioritizes the actions.

Do you understand the scale and complexity of completing just the first Block? If you fail to approach the Business Improvement in this way, **then you can be overwhelmed**. This was the opening word used in the first sentence of the section on **Russian Dolls.**

True Story: The Planning Manager for a large food manufacturer attempted to forecast and plan the future raw material and people requirements for the Business: he was unable to cope with this and had to leave the Company. At the time, he was trying to manage this in his head, without the use of a Master Schedule or Material Requirements Plan.

Move to Block 2: **'People - Forecast/Plan - Quantity'** - That's a new piece of flip-chart paper labelled 'Block 2' in the top left-hand corner, and list the **tools and actions** that are needed. Starting with a check of employees currently on the payroll, then where they live, which should help the management team to understand where the optimal location of their new premises should be to facilitate ease of transport to the site. Beginning to understand the inter-connections between Blocks: and its covers all aspects of a business. In Blocks 1 and 2, you should be listing legal, health and safety, ergonomics, recruitment and selection, training, business planning, management control systems (MCS) and contingency planning as a few of the subjects. From these, recruitment and selection training, MCS, are tools - the rest need to be on your action list.

Move to Block 3: **'People - Forecast/Plan - Time'** - If time is money, and the business closed late on Friday afternoon, then progress on the Improvement has to be **measured in hours.** Which means that your Tools and actions have to be measured in hours.

True Stories: Many Senior and Middle Managers struggle to measure time in hours: they prefer days or shifts, with reports and review meetings. Only once have I ever witnessed a senior person measure time in seconds - and their direct reports quickly got the 'time' message.

In the second story, the Boss held a daily update meeting with the whole management team at 8.00am sharp: and 'sharp' meant at exactly 8.00am. This came as quite a shock to most managers.

Here's a Tool that's not listed as one of the 29: critical path analysis. Now often overlooked and superseded by a myriad of software management tools, this remains a firm favourite to understand what absolutely has to be done and when.

By now, there's a clear pattern as to how the Cube is used: and here are some of the underlying reasons why:-

1.   Historically, all Business Improvements start with the original Idea / Improvement, and the thinking expands outwards from that point of origin. This seems like an almost flawless approach - the people who know best are the originators of the Business Improvement. Not when it comes to deploying that Improvement. **Thinking has to be PRIORITIZED** - People, Health & Safety first. On

countless occasions, people are an after-thought. Take Grenfell Tower, or Boeing's MCAS upgrade, or the British Rail Timetable upgrade, or many BIs that fail to put 'People' and the customer experience first.

2.   By starting at Block 1, it's necessary to involve organizational functions that deal with People - Human Resources in particular. And **succession planning** at every level in the Improvement is critical: if you lose the BI Leader, who replaces that person. Who will be a full-time member of the BI Team, or do you only need part-time members. Are all Department and Line Manager in agreement with the BI plan? So for the Cube can be fully completed, there has to be involvement from all other relevant specialist functions. It's an 'Open Door' policy that's needed.

3.   **Many business improvements are BAD**. They may have started off as brilliant ideas in isolation, but you need a Cube Team to sort the 'wheat from the chaff'. An article by Dave Logan illustrates the point. "The problem with most organizations is that they are governed by mediocre ideas." So says retired Hanover Insurance CEO Bill O'Brien in his book, 'Dance of Change'. *'In my almost 20 years of studying and consulting to organizations, as well as teaching their executives, I'm astonished at how bad ideas keep flowing into companies -- and how resistant most people are to letting them die. These ideas make companies weak, encourage employees to "quit and stay," crush innovation, and create cultures of despair. Like weeds, **bad ideas crowd out actual thinking** and need to be pulled up from the roots".* If it's a bad Business Improvement idea, kill it dead!

4.   **Cross-checking the facts.** Multi-skilled Teams recruited from different disciplines are often able to remove the 'bullshit' that is substituted for business facts.

5.   **Using the Cube approach is more comprehensive and inclusive** - there's a broader spectrum of knowledgeable opinions and facts that contribute to the BI upfront: it may appear that a lot of resources are being devoted at an early stage , but this often saves even more wasted effort spent reworking later on.

6.   And lastly **decision-making**. Experience has shown that many key decisions can be made early in a BI. They are often based on partial facts or opinions, and can have a major impact throughout the BI. Keep key decisions on the back burner until the last moment: wait until more facts and evidence is available, then decide with the Team.

Take the seven highlighted points above, and apply them to the case study. Remember that this BI is critical to the survival of the business - as the Authorities have closed the business down, then the next steps are 'make-or-break'. And this is how events unfolded:-

Thinking has to be PRIORITIZED - New processing / manufacturing location within 3 days, which meets all of the Authorities' Health and Safety requirements. Delete all options that don't meet these requirements: as **bad ideas** (in this case sites) **crowd out actual thinking**, then just focus on sites that meet the criteria. **Cross-check the facts** on the sites that qualify. **Using the Cube approach is more comprehensive and inclusive** and means that there are dozens of senior and middle managers getting 'suitable site data' - something that would normally be handled by just one or two senior managers in a business. Which meant that **decision-making** had to be almost immediate based on available facts and opinions. And the last point, **succession planning**, may not have seemed relevant at the time, but was in fact critical. There had to be a clear definition of who would take command should the current Bosses have to spend a protracted time with the Authorities. And who was needed to be the senior operations manager in the new premises once the physical transfer of the business had been made.

Apply the Cube approach: there are a myriad of 'things that have to be done' in very little time, and the Cube helps to **structure the thinking** to focus on 'what has to be done when'. So if it's finding a new premises, then it's 'doing a deal' with the owner in hours, not weeks or months, as would normally be the case.

The outcome was that the physical move took place over a weekend and the business was 'back in business' by 8.00am on Monday morning. Which means that we were able to process orders as well as meeting the Authorities' legal and statutory requirements. Most BIs are not this dramatic or urgent: but business survival can be a great motivator. The next true story seems more likely.

True Story: A large, high-tech manufacturer of computer hardware employed consultants to reduce the operating costs within one of their divisions. This goal was achieved within 11 weeks of starting the BI, and the financial benefit was agreed with the divisional and corporate accountants: annualized savings were at a 21:1 Return on Investment (ROI) against project cost-to-date. The corporate client closed the project, and was delighted that they had removed the extra costs that the divisional manager had built into his divisional budget. The unit cost of production was reduced by 22%.

All within 11 weeks from the project start. If this level of business improvement doesn't energize you into action, then nothing will. This level of results are deliverable: if you're the Boss, then you should be stretching your Team to achieve similar improvements. And if you are not, then you are failing in one of your business responsibilities. So blow the dust off your business dreams and get started NOW!

A TACTICAL REMINDER

This book is interspersed with *True Stories* amid a very clear preference for using Neuro-Linguistic Programming to effect improvement, together with a Boss who clearly understands what he or she wants from any business improvement. Take these management ingredients and frame the them within the Business Cube that provides **a structured and disciplined approach to thinking** about BIs.

The traditional approach to BI emphasises the functional areas that often require attention - sales and marketing, operations, logistics and customer service: the departmental structure that manages the Functions - management hierarchy, human resources, legal and even external consultants: and then replicates the business strengths and weaknesses in the BI Team.

Break the business improvement habits of a lifetime: start thinking and acting with the Boss and inside the Cube - as the title of the book says, it's all about 'Think Twice and Cutting Once'.

Not convinced yet: these are the latest Project Management performance indicators from several reputable sources, and summarized by Karine Tavrizyan of Crowdbotics[59]. As the Project Management format is the Business Improvement medium of choice for most businesses, then this survey is particularly relevant. 'The field of project management is changing, and it's changing faster than ever did. New techniques, frameworks, and tools are disrupting entrenched players and undoing long-held beliefs. But what is the impact of these changes? **How many projects fail, and why?** To answer these questions, I've compiled a comprehensive list of the latest project management statistics and gathered data points culled from dozens of studies for your reference.

Project Management Adoption Statistics: What is the adoption rate of project management software across organizations?

Only 58% of organizations fully understand the value of project management. Project Management Institute (PMI)

93% of organizations report using standardized project management practices. (PMI)

File sharing, time tracking, email integration, Gantt Charts, and budget management are the top five most used and requested features in project management software. (Capterra)

Only 22% of organizations use a PM software. 55% of organizations don't have access to real-time KPIs. As a result, 50% of respondents said that they spend one or more days to manually collate project reports — highlighting the immense productivity gains on offer by using project management software. (Wellingtone)

Between 2017 and 2018, the percentage of organizations using spreadsheets to manage their agile projects dropped from 74% to 67%. Instead, these organizations moved to specialized PM tools. (VersionOne)

77% of high-performing projects use project management software. Despite its impact, adoption rates for PM software remains low (22%). 66% of project managers say that they would use PM software more extensively if they had adequate support from their organization. (Hive)

Project Management Performance Statistics

What is the average failure rate of a project? Among successful projects, what factors have the biggest impact on success?

Project performance has been rising globally. In 2018, nearly 70% of projects met their original goals or business intent, while nearly 60% were completed within the original budget. Both these figures are up from 62% and 50% respectively in 2016. (PMI)

IT projects are notoriously difficult to manage. A survey found that the average IT project overran its budget by 27%. **Moreover, at least one in six IT projects turns into a "black swan" with a cost overrun of 200% and a schedule overrun of 70%.** Harvard business Review (HBR)

Among IT projects, failure rate corresponds heavily to project size. **An IT project with a budget over $1M is 50% more likely to fail than one with a budget below $350,000. For such large IT projects, functionality issues and schedule overruns are the top two causes of failure (at 22% and 28% respectively).** (Gartner)

A PwC study of over 10,640 projects found that only 2.5% of companies complete their projects 100% successfully. The rest either failed to meet some of their original targets or missed the original budget or deadlines. These failures extract a heavy cost — failed IT projects alone cost the United States $50-$150B in lost revenue and productivity. (Gallup)

Among IT projects, project performance varies significantly. **While software projects have an average cost overrun of 66%, the same figure for non-software projects is 43%. However, 133% of non-software projects fail to meet their stated benefits, compared to just 17% for software**

projects. (McKinsey Consultants)

17% of IT projects can go so bad that they can threaten the very existence of the company. (McKinsey Consultants)

We can do better than this! **Or can we?**

References & Sources for the 'Tactical Reminder' section:
'PMI: Pulse of the profession 2018', Project Management Institute
'Delivering large-scale IT projects on time, on budget, and on value', McKinsey Consultants.
'The cost of bad project management', Gallup
'Survey shows why projects fail', Gartner
The State of Project Management: Annual survey 2018, Wellingtone
'PMI: Pulse of the profession' 2017', Project Management Institute
Why your IT project may be riskier than you think', Harvard Business Review
Project Management user research report, Capterra

Name me a famous Business Improvement Manager currently working in the UK: well then, the most well known one in the world. Struggling to name anybody (if you're married, it could be your partner managing the household economy!). On a more serious note, there are a few managers driving business improvements in the UK at the present time that you should be aware of. They will have a significant impact on our national future.

Let's take a further look at the example of Crossrail[60] mentioned in Chapter 2 - this is the improvement and extension to the Transport for London[61] (TfL) network in London, which has been bedevilled by cost overruns and delays in completion. The same Project Manager who oversaw part of the ongoing Crossrail project as **Strategic Projects Director,** is now leading the HS2 railway development in the UK since March 2017. As the Chief Executive, he seems to have absorbed the role of Chief Project Manager - with a host of 'Project Manager' titles to support this enormous engineering assignment. [From a UK transport network perspective, HS2 is a new railway line and infrastructure better connecting the North and South regions of the UK: so it's a massive improvement on the present network].

This book proposes that the performance of the **No.1 Boss** is critical to the success of any BI: so the recruitment and selection of the person at the top of the HS2 organization would be of fundamental importance. Comparing 'Crossrail' with 'HS2' is simply a matter of scaling up from the current Crossrail budget of £18.7b. in 2020 to compare with the current total HS2 budget of over £107b. for all Phases of the planned route. If you examine the fundamental reasons for the Crossrail budget overruns and time delays, then the head of the HS2 project [Mark Thurston] nails one of the major issues in an interview with **New Civil Engineer's** publication. He says, *'There is still a wider corporate discipline and a **project management discipline of not starting to build until we get fully designed'.** So the Crossrail project was still being designed as it was being built: HS2 started off in exactly the same way: do you think there's a problem with this approach? As Thurston commented regarding the design and build of the new Crossrail stations,..'**but for a range reasons there's something not gone quite right there'.**

If the **No.1 Boss** is critical to the success of a BI (and both Crossrail and HS2 are regarded as Drivers of Business Improvement in the UK), then the **Business Cube** is the second innovation that's needed. This approach would provide an in-depth assessment with a **Full Business Plan** based on the latest costings and projected benefits from delivering HS2. At the moment, the HS2 Team are working with the **Current Stages of HS2 Programme** as laid out on the next page.

Although fairly succinct, it clearly shows the **Full Business Plan** only being completed just before the **Construction** phase: until that point, all decision-making has been based on the **Outline Business Plan.** And that's the first fundamental flaw: the Business Cube approach would involve a complete understanding of the scope and complexity of the project before any work is undertaken. The second flaw lies in the **Construction** phase, and was highlighted by an article (Oct. 2020, Rob Horgan) in the **New Civil Engineer's** publication, which states, 'The new system is similar to the process implemented throughout **Crossrail's six-week blockade during the summer, which resulted in 1,235 of a total 1,286 milestones being completed.** The meeting notes add: **"A 'blockade mentality' is being implemented for the management of the stations programme.**

Before the **Construction** phase: until that point, all decision-making has been based on the **Outline Business Plan.** And that's the first fundamental flaw: the Business Cube approach would involve a complete understanding of the scope and complexity of the project before any work is undertaken. The second flaw lies in the **Construction** phase, and was highlighted by an

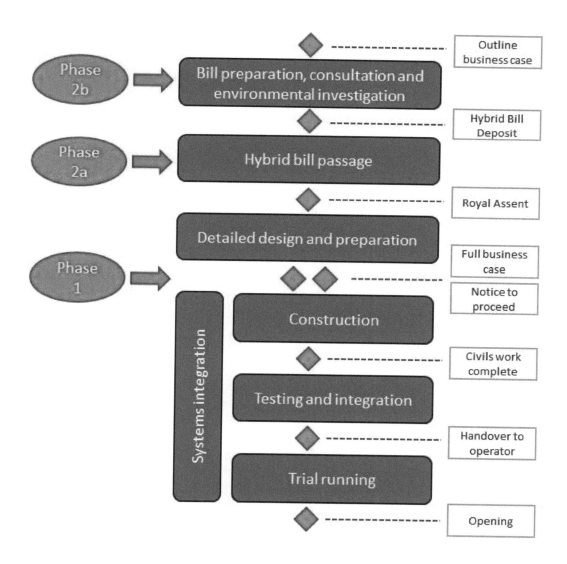

Current Stages of the HS2 Programme - Courtesy of the Oakervee Report[62]

57

article (Oct. 2020, Rob Horgan) in the **New Civil Engineer's** publication, which states, 'The new system is similar to the process implemented throughout **Crossrail's six-week blockade during the summer, which resulted in 1,235 of a total 1,286 milestones being completed.** The meeting notes add: **"A 'blockade mentality' is being implemented for the management of the stations programme. "This involves knowing the scope of works remaining, measuring performance against this in a detailed and simple way, and having frequent intervention-based management meetings to resolve issues and re-plan works as soon as deviation from targets occurs**. Together, these will provide greater control over the systems works remaining and will ensure there is alignment between all stakeholders'. This is called active business improvement (or Project) Management.

Mister James Wren (25 Oct, 2020 at 2:33 pm.) commented on this article in the same publication two days later. 'This involves knowing the scope of works remaining, measuring performance against this in a detailed and simple way, and having frequent intervention-based management meetings to resolve issues and re-plan works as soon as deviation from targets occurs.' **Gosh, that's a new concept!!! We used to call it good programme management and did it as a weekly routine!**

From personal experience, I could add further comments, but it's not necessary. For those unsure as to what Mr. Wren is referring, please watch this video:-

BBC[64] - **https://www.bbc.co.uk/iplayer** - 'Grand Designs' - 'A 21st Century Answer to the Roman Villa: Revisited' (Series 5: Episode 9, Belfast, Northern Ireland, 2 November 2005).** This is Belfast, one of the great cities of the industrial revolution, and home to Thomas and Dervla O'Hare. (*They've lived here for 18 years, and although they still love their tiny cottage for its compactness, they're about to build something much, much bigger. They're building a 21st century answer to the Roman villa, with a copper roof, glass and concrete walls and vast amounts of living space all arranged around a central courtyard).*

This is probably the finest example of Active Project Management being demonstrated real-time through the building of a 'replacement' house - it may not be a BI (more of a residential improvement (RI)), but it's certainly a bigger and better house, delivered on-time and in-budget!

Crossrail is a London transport upgrade that was not adequately thought through before construction work started. It then suffered from an inadequate management control system that allowed the project to drift in terms of time and costs. So when some of the engineering problems began to surface, particularly regarding the new London stations, then there was not the capability or drive to quickly correct the problems. The Strategic Projects Director for Crossrail is now the CEO of HS2 since March 2017. So how is HS2 going to be different?

The start of HS2 has been much the same as Crossrail in terms of in-depth understanding of engineering, costings and the project approach. That leaves the 'Active Management' aspect of the the Construction phase of HS2 - and that is a big question-mark. What is clear is that HS2 is being **thought twice**, probably before **cutting once.** Admittedly, this is a few year's overdue, but better late than never! And for 'Active Management' at HS2: why are Crossrail managing with a 'Blockade Mentality' when HS2 are not?

The same methodology can be applied to any size or type of business. So a one-person business (sole trader) can spend a few hours at the beginning of the financial year to think through the improvements that need to happen in their business, using the Cube of course! Or there's a very large improvement project to upgrade the UK rail network (HS2), where you would probably involve 100s of their most knowledgeable managers and employees for 6 months prior to any work starting on the project itself. Seems like an enormous investment for very little visible output? Not when you consider the thousands of hours of rework on Crossrail costing extra billions of pounds.

Notes:

Page No.:

1. Think Twice, Cut Once[1] - Courtesy of rebuildingyou.com - taking time to *really* think things through.

3. Russian Dolls[2] - set of hollow wooden figures, each of which splits in half to contain the next smallest figure, down to the smallest Doll.

3. Structured Thinking[3] - https://www.analyticsvidhya.com - Structured thinking is a process of putting a framework to an unstructured problem.

4. Profitability[4] - https://www.myaccountingcourse.com is the ability of a company to use its resources to generate revenues in excess of its expenses.

4. Resources[5] - https://www.collinsdictionary.com - the resources of an organization or person are the materials, money, and other things that they have and can use in order to function properly.

4. Standards[6] - A standard is a level of quality or achievement (for *Safety/Quality, Quantity and Time*)

4. Management Systems[7] - https://www.yourdictionary.com/management-system - The leadership and control within an organization.

5. Cube Lite[8] - The 'working' version of the Business Cube, used on a daily/weekly basis to keep the BI and Improvement Team informed and aligned.

6. Matryosha[9] Doll - The Russian language term for this type of Doll.

6. GUM[10] Store - Large department store.

6. Recent Article[11] - By Renoir Consulting.

7. Ogilvy[12], David - Founder of Ogilvy & Mather, and known as the "Father of Advertising".

7. McCullen[13], Aiden - Businessman and retired Ireland national rugby union team player.

8. Weinstock[14], Arnold - British industrialist and businessman known for making General Electric Company one of Britain's most profitable companies.

8. Brummer, Alex[15] - British economics commentator, working as a journalist, editor, and author. He has been the City Editor of the Daily Mail.

12. Rubik Cube[16] - Is a 3-D combination puzzle invented in 1974 by Hungarian sculptor and professor of architecture Ernő Rubik.

13. Call Centre[17] - Is a centralised office used for receiving or transmitting a large volume of enquiries by telephone.

15. Crossrail[18] - Is a railway construction project under way mainly in central London.

17. NHS[19] - British National Health Service.

18. NLP[20] - Neuro-linguistic Programming - is a pseudo-scientific approach to communication, personal development, and psychotherapy.

18. LLM[21] - Logical Levels Model - These 'logical levels' used in Neuro-Linguistic Programming (NLP), and provide a helpful structure for looking at what's happening in any individual, group or organisation.

19. Analytics Vidhya[22] - https://www.analyticsvidhya.com - website devoted to data science.

19. Kepner-Tregoe[23] - https://www.kepner-tregoe.com - Consulting firm focusing on training and problem solving.

20. The Pyramid Principle[24] - will show you how to communicate your ideas clearly and succinctly. The author is Barbara Minto.

20. The McKinsey Approach[25] - https://www.mckinsey.com - McKinsey & Company are a global management consulting firm, using the 'McKinsey 7S Model' as a tool to analyze a company's "organizational design."

20. Actknowledge[26] - https://www.actknowledge.org - understanding and making social change initiatives work.

20. Systematic Inventive Thinking[27] (SIT) - https://www.sitsite.com - teaches you how to maintain a competitive edge through efficiency and productivity.

20. The art of structured thinking and analyzing[28] - K. Jain
https://www.analyticsvidhya.com/blog/2013/06/art-structured-thinking-analyzing

22. DMAIC[29] - a data-driven improvement cycle used for improving, optimizing and stabilizing business processes and designs. The DMAIC improvement cycle is **the core tool used to drive Six Sigma projects.**

23. Stephen Covey[30] - https://stephencovey.com - an American educator, author and businessman.

23. Blocks and Tools[31] - from the Business Cube - 27 Blocks and 29 Tools.

26. Reward Triangle[32] - a BI Tool of NBJ Business Solutions Ltd.

27. Master Schedule[33] - a BI Tool that matches the 'People required' with the 'Hours Worked Required' - the link between Work Volume and People Hours Available, and Activity Based Costing.

28. MRP[34] (Material Requirement Planning) - Businesses use material requirements-planning systems to estimate quantities of raw materials and schedule their deliveries.

29. 8 Types of Waste[35] - The original 7 'Wastes' (Muda) were developed by Taiichi Ohno, the Chief Engineer at Toyota, as part of the Toyota Production System (TPS). By adding Skill's Waste, the 7 8. (Transportation, Inventory, Motion, Waiting, Overproduction, Extra-processing and Defects) become eight.

29. Self-directed work teams[36] - (SDWTs) - are a group of skilled people working toward a common goal. It takes collaboration to a new level as it ensures that there are different skills and abilities within the same team.

36. Process Framework[37] - https://www.seguetech.com/services/application-development - the Segue Process Framework (SPF) adapts to the scope of the project and the technologies which best suit customers' requirements.

36.- Brilliant factory[38] - A concept factory by GE: it involves machines that are embedded with sensors and connected to the Industrial Internet. The factory uses GE's Predix software platform to stream data - over secure links - into the cloud for analysis. Insights are then sent back to engineers with suggestions on how to improve operations. https://www.ge.com/news/reports/new-brilliant-factory-offers-blueprint-north-american-manufacturing

38. Software methodologies[39] - https://www.developer.com/mgmt/slideshows/10-top-programming-methodologies.html - Top ten software methodologies.

40. Alistair Mant[40] is an international authority on leadership and talent development. Currently the Adjunct Professor at Swinburne University of Technology in Melbourne. His grounding in complex systems work came from the Tavistock Institute in London.

41. Using the Cube[41] - Brings together the key elements for a successful BI: the Russian Dolls, the Business Cube, and the Logical Levels Model from Neuro-Linguistic Programming. BI Tool used by NBJ Business Solutions Ltd.

44. FMEA[42] - Failure Modes Effects Analysis' - is an inductive reasoning (forward logic) single point of failure analysis and is a core task in reliability engineering, safety engineering and quality engineering.

44. Brainstorming[43] - is a group creativity technique which offers to find a conclusion for a specific problem by gathering a list of ideas spontaneously contributed by team members.

44. Creative thinking[44] - is a skill which lets you consider things from a fresh perspective.

44. Mind-mapping[45] - is a technique that creates a diagram to visually organize information.

44. Checklist[46] - A checklist is a list of all the things that you need to do, information that you want to find out, or things that you need to take somewhere, which you make in order to ensure that you do not forget anything.

44. Six Thinking Hats[47] - written by Dr. Edward de Bono. 'Six Thinking Hats' provides a means for groups to plan thinking processes in a detailed and cohesive way, and in doing so to think together more effectively.

44. Lateral thinking[48] - Lateral thinking is a manner of solving problems using an indirect and creative approach via reasoning.

44. The Ishikawa Tree[49] (Fishbone) - Ishikawa diagrams are causal diagrams to show the potential causes of a specific event.

44. SWOT analysis[50] - is a strategic planning technique used to help a person or organization identify strengths, weaknesses, opportunities, and threats related to business competition or project planning.

44. Stair-step critical thinking model[51] - content knowledge/problem solving skills Identifying the unstructured nature of the problem.

44. Flexible thinking[52] - A critical thinking process when the learner remains open to multiple possibilities, ideas, or hypotheses, particularly when information and evidence is still being gathered.

44. Structured thinking[53] - is having a structure to our thoughts. Structured thinking was developed

by Barbara Minto (McKinsey & Co.) and Andy Shaw, the creator of 'A Bug Free Mind'. https://members.abugfreemind.com. The Process was created to teach people 'How To Think', **NOT** 'What To Think'.

46. TSB[54] (Trustee Savings Bank) - Founded in 1810, TSB Bank plc is a retail and commercial bank in the United Kingdom and a subsidiary of Sabadell Group. TSB Bank operates a network of 536 branches across England, Scotland and Wales but has not had a presence in Northern Ireland since 1991.

46. Sabadell[55] - Banco de Sabadell, S.A. is a Spanish multinational financial services company with headquarters in Alicante, Spain.

48. Grenfell Tower Fire[56] - https://www.grenfelltowerinquiry.org.uk - for the latest update regarding this tragedy.

49. High-speed train line project[57] (HS2) - High Speed 2 is a planned high speed railway in the United Kingdom, with its first phase under construction and future stages awaiting approval. For the latest update - https://www.hs2.org.uk.

50. Patisserie Valerie[58] - is a chain of cafés that operates in the United Kingdom.

55. Crowdbotics[59] - https://www.crowdbotics.com - this company builds scalable apps for businesses.

56. Crossrail[60] - https://www.crossrail.co.uk - is Crossrail is a railway construction project under way mainly in central London. Its aim is to provide a high-frequency suburban passenger service crossing London from west to east, to be branded the 'Elizabeth' line.

56. Transport for London[61] (TfL) - Transport for London is a local government body responsible for the transport system in Greater London.

57. Oakervee Report[62] - https://www.gov.uk/government/publications/oakervee-review-of-hs2 - The review was asked to assemble and test all the existing evidence in order to allow the Prime Minister, the Secretary of State for Transport and the government to make properly-informed decisions.

58. New Civil Engineer[63] - https://www.newcivilengineer.com - is the monthly magazine for members of the UK Institution of Civil Engineers.

58. BBC[64] (British Broadcasting Corporation) - https://www.bbc.com - is a public service broadcaster based in the UK.

Key Term's Index:

Bibliography (Alphabetical by Surname)
Published Sources and Recommended Reading

Allen, David, *Getting Things Done*, March 2017.

Anderson, David, *Design for Manufacturability: How to Use Concurrent Engineering to Rapidly Develop Low-Cost, High-Quality Products for Lean Production,* 2006, Productivity Press.

Beddoes-Jones, Fiona, *Relationship Strategies that Work!,* 1999.

Berenson, Alex, *The Number,* 2003.

Bevan, Judi, *The Rise and Fall of Marks and Spencer,* 2002.

Blenko Marcia, Michael Mankins, Paul Rogers, *Decide & Deliver,* Bain & Co., 2010.

Collins, Jim, *Good to Great,* 2001.

Cruver, Brian, *Enron: Anatomy of Greed,* 2002.

Dobelli, Rolf, *The Art of Thinking Clearly*, 2013.

Frierstein, Mitch, *Planet Ponzi,* 2012.

Garratt, Bob, *The Fish rots from the Head,* 1996.

Geneen Harold, Alvin Moscow, *Managing,* 1984.

George Michael, David Rowlands, Mark Price, John Maxey, *Lean 6 Sigma Pocket Toolbook,* 2005.

Goldratt, Eliyahu, *Theory of Constraints,* January 1999.

Goldratt, Eliyahu, *The Goal,* 1984.

Goleman, Daniel, *Emotional Intelligence Why it Can Matter More Than IQ, Sept* 1996.

Ghoshal, Sumantra & Bartlett, Christopher, *The Individualized Corporation,* 1988.

Hirano, Hiroyuki, *5 Pillars of the Visual Workplace,* 1995.

Honey, Peter, *50 Cautionary Tales for Managers,* 2006.

Horowitz, Ben, *The Hard thing about Hard Things,* 2014.

James, Oliver, *Office Politics,* 2013.

Jensen, Bill, *The New Competitive Advantage,* 2000.

Krogerus, Mikael & Tschappler, Roman, *The Decision Book,* 2011.

Lewis, Gareth, *The Mentoring Manager,* 1996.

Lewis, Michael, *Liar's Poker,* 1989.

Mant, Alistair, *Leaders we Deserve,* 1983.

Martyr, Tony, *Why Projects Fail: Nine Laws for Success,* 2018.

Mauboussin, Michael, *Think Twice,* 2013.

McLean Bethany and Peter Elkind, *The Smartest Guys in the Room,* 2003.

Mintzberg, Henry, *Structure in Fives,* June 1992.

Moore, P G, *Basic Operational Research,* 1968.

Norton Bob , Cathy Smith, *Understanding Management Gurus,* 1998.

O'Shea James and Charles Madigan, *Dangerous Company,* 1999.

Osono Emi, Norohiko Shimizu, Hirotaka Takeuchi, *Extreme Toyota,* 2008.

Papke, Edgar, *True Alignment,* Amacom, 2014.

Pink, Daniel, *When,* January 2018.

Schonberger, Richard, *Building a Chain of Customers,* 1990.

Singer, Mark, *Funny Money,* 1985.

Smith, Jay, *How Jeff Bezos Built an E-Commerce Empire: The Unwritten Story of Amazon.com,* April 2018.

Sorkin, Andrew Ross, *Too Big to Fail,* 2009.

Taleb, Nassim Nicholas, *The Black Swan*, 2007.

Thomas, C William, *The Rise and Fall of Enron*, March/April 2002.

University of Sheffield, HR Dep't., *On Recruitment and Selection*, 2018.

Articles (Alphabetical by Surname)

Agrawal, Jyoti, *8 Benefits of Blockchain to Industries Beyond Cryptocurrency*, January 2018.

Ambler, Scott, *The Disciplined Agile Consortium*, Scott W. Ambler + Associates, 2014.

Andrulis, Jeremy, *How Are You Maximising Return on People Investment?*, Aon, January 2017.

Anon, *Building a best in class liquidity management structure*, Treasury Today, January 2017.

Anon, *Self-Directed Work Teams*, MBASkool.com, 2018.

Anon, www.sixleansigma.com, Lean Six Sigma, 2018.

Anon, *How to determine critical customer requirements*, Lean Six Sigma, July 2017.

Anon, *Understanding Agile Project Management from Lean Six Sigma Perspective*, Lean Six Sigma, October 2016.

Anon, *Return on Investment – ROI*, My Accounting Course, 2018.

Anon, *Klipfolio is a cloud analytics platform for building business intelligence dashboards and reports for your team or clients*, Klipfolio, November 2018.

Anon, *How General Electric Used Six Sigma to Transform Their Company*, MySixSigmatrainer.com

Anon, *Is Six Sigma Dead at GE?*, October 2006.

Anon, *The Importance of Cash Management to Small Business Success:Managing Assets, Cashflow and Liquidity for Healthy Returns*, The Balance Small Business, 2018.

Anon, *www.leanproduction.com/short-interval-control.html*, Vorne Industries Inc., 2011 - 2018.

Arrington, Michael,*There is a difference between evil and just being absurdly profitable*, Oct. 2009.

Bassi, Laurie: McMurrer, Daniel, *How's your Return on People*, HBR, March 2004.

Baum, Dan, *8 Most Important Social Media Marketing Trends in 2018 to Watch*, January 2018.

Beyer, Philip, *Why Lean Fails 98% of the Time? The Answer*, System 100, April 2017.

Bisk, *Is Logistics the Same as Supply Chain Management?*, Michigan State University, 2018.

Breen, Jim, *'Fully driverless combine harvester by 2024'*, Agriland, August 2017.

Brian, Ray, *Effective, Low-Cost Real-Time Location System (& 5 Alternative Technologies)*, January 2018.

Broni-Mensah, Louise, *'Excellence isn't an act, it's a habit'*, December 2018.

Buerkle, Tom, *G.E.'s New C.E.O. Risks Repeating History*, New York Times, November 2018.

Burgess, Kate, *Collapse of Carillion*, January 2018.

Capterra, Project Management user research report.

Croce Annalisa, Jose Marti, Samuel Murtinu, *The Impact of venture capital on the productivity growth of European entrepreneurial firms*, July 2013.

Cheto, Lauden, *Management Control Systems*, KLM Consult, June 2015.

Cummings, Douglas et al., *Governmental and independent venture capital investments in Europe: A firm-level performance analysis*, 2016.

Dougal, *CEO Secrets: Recruit people 'better than you'*, BBC, August 2015.

Duhigg, Charles, *Want to be more productive? Think deeper'*, Opinion, Director, May 2016.

Dougal, *CEO Secrets: Recruit people 'better than you'*, BBC, August 2015.

Figliolino, Venanzio, *Kaizen vs Kaikaku*, August 2015.

Forland, Chris, Scott Grunwald, Miranda Pilrose, *Parts, People, Process: The Winning Formula for Emerson Turnarounds and Certified Services,* 2018.

Florentine, Sharon, *IT project success rates finally improving,* February 2017.

Gallup, *The cost of bad project management.*

Gartenstein, Debra, *The Advantages of Just-in-Time Inventory Systems,* June 28, 2018.

Gifford, Jonny, *Performance management: an introduction,* CIPD, September 2018.

Gifford, Jonny, *Could do better? What works in performance management,* CIPD, December 2016.

Gosport Independent Panel, *Gosport War Memorial Hospital,* June 2018.

Guardian et al., *RBS escapes action over controversial GRG unit,* July 2018.

Hannabarger, Charles Buchman, Frederick, Economy,Peter: *Balanced Scorecard Strategy For Dummies,* April 2013.

Harvard Business Review, *Why your IT project may be riskier than you think.*

Harvard Business School, *Compliance Chain Analysis,* February 2016.

Hash Management Services Ltd., *8 Wastes in Lean Manufacturing,* 2018.

Higgins, Chad, *Lean Six Sigma Certification is a Waste of Time! Or is it?,* May 2018.

Holmes, Tyrone: *Ten Characteristics of a High Performance Work Team, T.A.H. Performance Consultants, Inc.,* undated.

Hooda, Saurabh, *5 ways HR will be affected by Artificial Intelligence,* People Matters, November 2018.

House of Commons, *Business, Energy and Industrial Strategy and Work and Pensions Committees (Carillion),* 2018.

House of Commons, Briefing Paper, *The Collapse of Carillion, No. 8206,* March 2018.

House of Commons, Transport Committee, *Rail Timetable Changes, HC 1163,* June 2018.

House of Commons, Treasury Committee, HC 1009, *Service Disruption at TSB,* June 2018.

Hyacinth, Brigette, *Micromanagement make BEST PEOPLE Quit!,* July 2018.

IBM / CIO Leadership Office, *Update for TSB Board,* April 2018.

Infrastructure and Projects Authority, *UK Government,* 2011

Jacobs, Katie, *Is Psychometric testing still fit for purpose?,* February 2018.

Karapetrovic, Stanislav, *Strategies for the integration of management systems and standards, 2002.*

Lemonis, Marcus, *The Profit,* 2018.

Local Government Association, *High Impact Change Model: Managing Transfers of Care, 2018.*

Lucidchart Content Team, *What the Waterfall Project Management Methodology Can (and Can't) Do for You,* August 2017.

MacDonald, Lynne: *What Is a Self-Managed Team?,* Chron., June, 2018.

Malik, Danish, *Role of Artificial Intelligence in Agriculture,* DigitalOcean, July 2018.

Martin, Gary, *Pot Stirrers and blame Gamers,* May 2018.

McBride, Carter, *Definition of Gross Profit Margin,* Chron, Hearst Newspapers 2018.

McGraw, Karen, *Improving Project Success Rates with Better Leadership,* PM Times, November 2018.

McKinsey, *Delivering large-scale IT projects on time, on budget, and on value.*

Mieritz, Lars, *Gartner, Survey shows why projects fail,* 2012.

Mindtools, *7 Ways to Use Office Politics Positively,* 2016.

Mintzberg, Henry & Gratton, Lynda, *Top Thinkers,* 2018.

Mitchell, Adam, *Kaizen, Kaikaku & Kakushin – what's the difference?* January 2018.

Monaghan, Angela, *Timeline of trouble: how TSB IT meltdown unfolded,* June 2018.

Montag, Ali, *This is Jeff Bezos' 3-question test for new Amazon employees,* August 2018.

Moore, James, The Independent, *RBS & GRG,* January 2018.

Myers Briggs, *Personality Types*, 1948.

National Cyber Security Centre, 2016.

Nelson, Robert, *The Leaders Use of Informal Rewards and Reward Systems in Obtaining Organizational Goals*, November 1993.

Oakervee, Douglas, *Oakervee Review*, 2019

Page, Bob, *Hoshin Planning: Making the Strategic Plan Work*, isixsigma.com, 2000 - 2018.

Parikh, Tej, *Lifting the Long Tail: The Productivity challenge through the eyes of small business leaders'* Institute of Directors, IoD, (October 2018).

Parkinson, Mark, CIPD, *A Head for Hiring*, 2015.

Persona People Management Ltd., *The Five Key Factors*, 2018.

PMI: Pulse of the profession 2018', Project Management Institute

Porter, Sarah, *Apple*, 2018.

Process Excellence (PEX) – 7 companies that forever changed the face of process excellence

2014.

Renoir Ltd., *9 Rules of project management*, 2018.

Reynolds, Paul, *A scheme to increase profitability in entrepreneurial SMEs.*, 2018.

Rockwell, Patrick, *When to use waterfall methodology*, August 2017.

Shaw, Dougal, *CEO Secrets: Recruit people 'better than you'*, BBC, August 2015.

Silverman, Lori: Propst, Annabeth, *Ensuring Success: A Model For Self-Managed Teams*, Partners for Progress and Fuller & Propst Associates, 1996.

Storey, Nate, *What are some applications of AI in the field of agriculture?*, May 2016.

Sullivan, Bob, *Agile, waterfall, Brooks' Law, and 94% failure rates — there's lots to learn from HealthCare.gov troubles*, Bobsullivan.net, October 2013.

Stanton, Daniel, *Measuring Supply Chain Processes*, February 2018.

Strom, John, *Maximizing Your ROPI - Return on Your People Investment*, January 2017.

Swartout, Donna, *Self-Directed Teams: Definition, Advantages & Disadvantages*, Study.com, 2018.

Templer, Klaus, *Personality and Individual Differences*, April 2018.

Tesco, *Strategic Report*, 2018.

Wellingtone, *The State of Project Management: Annual survey*, 2018

Williams, Phillip, *Zero Defects: What Does It Achieve? What Does It Mean?*, ISixSigma, 2018.

Wolfson, Rachel, *Diversifying Data With Artificial Intelligence And Blockchain Technology*, Forbes, November 2018.

Zebra.com, *Factory of the Future*, 2018.

Definitions inside the 'Business Cube'

RESOURCES

People The ***people*** that staff and operate a business.

Parts ***Parts,*** as used in a 'Production Part Approval Process', where 'all customer engineering design specification requirements are properly understood by the supplier and that the process has the potential to produce parts consistently meeting these requirements during an actual production run at the defined production rate.'

Process A ***process*** is a set of activities that interact to achieve a result.

Products ***Products***, as the totality of goods that a company makes available; output.

Services ***Services***, as the providing or a provider of activities required by customers.

STANDARDS

Safety ***Safety*** is the freedom from danger or risk of injury in business or at work.
Quality is the degree or standard of excellence.

Quantity ***Quantity*** refers to the specified or indefinite number or amount.

Time ***Time*** refers to a number, as of years, days, or minutes, representing such an interval.

MANAGEMENT SYSTEMS

Systems ***Management control systems*** are the formal and informal structures put in place by a Management control systems are the formal and informal.

Forecast ***Forecasting*** refers to the ability of a business to try to figure out what is coming along in the future by using information available today.

Planning ***Business Planning*** encompasses all the goals, strategies and actions that you envision taking to ensure your business's survival, prosperity, and growth.

Report ***Reporting*** refers to both "the public reporting of operating and financial data by a business enterprise," and "the regular provision of information to decision-makers within an organization to support them in their work."

Review ***Reviewing*** financial data analysis that provides assurance that the business is performing according to the Business Plan.

Postscript

Two postscripts: one is on a professional level, and the other is personal. Here goes.

On a professional level, I've tried to disprove the underlying themes that leadership and the Cube are the key ingredients to a successful and sustainable Business Improvement. Reviewing the current status of Business Improvements in the UK, most have been negatively impacted by the COVID 19 outbreak. But before the pandemic struck, the UK was struggling: as Julia Kollewe wrote in 'The Guardian' (2nd January 2020), *'The UK economy ended 2019 in stagnation, under pressure from long-term uncertainty, mounting business costs and a global economic slowdown. The British Chambers of Commerce's (BCC) latest quarterly economic snapshot, based on a poll of 6,500 firms across the country in November 2019, painted a gloomy picture of the economy at the end of the last decade'.* So the scene is set for 2020, and it's difficult to extrapolate future Business Improvements in the UK with a background of the current pandemic.

Rather like the new COVID 19 vaccines, one understands exactly what works by experimentation and trial-and-error. The same logic applies to business improvements: only by experimenting with Leadership development and using the Cube methodology are you going to discover that this approach can work for you and your Company, and can consistently deliver significant business improvements.

Lastly, on a professional basis, all the errors and omissions in this book are solely the responsibility of the author.

On a personal note, on the morning of the 22nd November 1974, I started to learn about how to manage business change. During the previous evening, the 'Tavern in the Town' pub in Birmingham, England was bombed, and, having been in there that evening, I understood what luck was all about. The pub was also located directly opposite the Birmingham branch of British Home Stores, where I was working as a Departmental Manager. So from being the largest and busiest Branch in the retail chain, we now had very few customers: similar to the present situation for High Street retailing in 2020 UK.

During the past 46 years, there have been a few lessons learned. And the first lesson was the Business Cube, developed over several years to manage a mountain of information that came from working many assignments on my own, with very tight deadlines and a few aggressive Bosses. If you think that being a professional business improvement manager is the working life for you, then please, *think twice so that you only have to cut once.*

Acknowledgements

In a working life, there are a few people that you work with and learn from who leave a lasting impression on your thinking. In chronological order, this book is dedicated to Nicholas Wethmar, Manager at British Home Stores in 1974, who showed me how to manage a crisis in the aftermath of a bomb explosion. He also said that 'everything you do today should have been done yesterday', a quote that has stuck in my mind for decades. Rick Chandler for tactical management: Jan Metzger for some brilliant technical work with a very difficult Client over many months: Ray Mills for demonstrating the power of systems within any business that needs to improve performance: Martyn Webber for support and guidance over a six year period: and Lai Phan for some excellent business improvements in very difficult circumstances.

In a professional life, there may be a few opportunities that offer a chance to develop different skill sets. Working alone on several BIs. meant I had to be creative about how to deliver the Client's requirements: that's when the Business Cube evolved, first as a box, then pyramid, and lastly in a Cube format. And then the Implementation Model developed from the need to use a training and development approach that could be rolled out quickly and effectively by just one manager. First came a multi-level training model, then the Implementation Model. Pleased to say my bosses often stayed away from my assignments and their Clients. Two reasons: my bosses were never sure how to achieve the BI targets themselves, so they delegated to a stand-alone manager who they could blame if the BI failed. And secondly, they never showed any interest in new tools/techniques/models: I guess if you already know everything, there's no need to learn anything more.

And some words for today's BI leaders. There's never been a better time to improve your business, or manage somebody's else's business more effectively and efficiently. And if you believe that 'Brexit' and 'Covid-19' are hampering BI initiatives, or the benefits are less than they were, then think about this:-

*'I make observations, having come from the oil and gas world, that we really have **construction projects in infrastructure that look the same today as they did 40 years ago.** There is a huge opportunity to use modern methods of construction and tools that will bring significant improvements in productivity. **I am not talking about marginal percentages, but 30%, 40% improvement**.... You will have to see that step change in productivity and take hours out of the construction of our projects.'* (Nick Smallwood, CEO of The Infrastructure and Projects Authority, giving evidence to the Transport Committee on major transport infrastructure projects: appraisal and delivery, Wednesday 12 May 2021).

Now construction projects can be business improvement initiatives: so the same thinking can apply in both cases. So I would wish Mr Smallwood the best of luck in the quest to improve performance in public and privately funded infrastructure improvements in the UK: and I acknowledge that this need to improve has prompted the writing of this book. And I hope you're inspired to explore the subject of business improvements in more depth.

2. The Russian Dolls

by Nick Jones

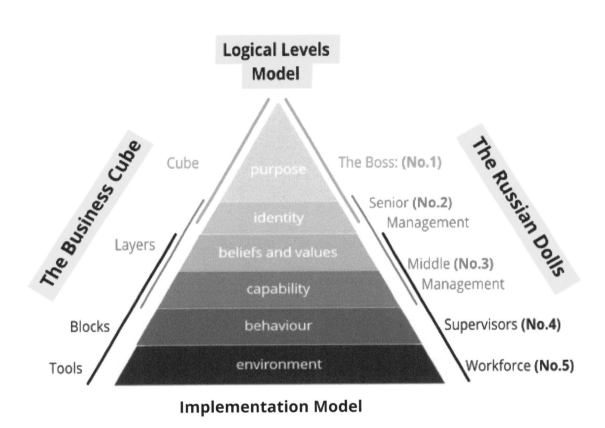

Preface

If you've taken the time to read, or just flick through, the first Section ('Think Twice, Cut Once') about business improvement, then you will have realised that Leadership[1] is a key ingredient for delivering successful Improvements. In fact, it is **'Business Improvement Critical'** - so we need to develop our understanding of the most effective forms of leadership that deliver the optimum results.

And there's no doubt that the subject of Leadership has generated a swathe of books and material in recent decades. *'Counting all formats, Amazon offers over 100,000 books with the word "leadership" in the title',* as of January 2021: and leadership books[2] are published at a rate of 4 per day. Why the fascination with this topic?

Probably because it's an open subject. Which means that any person with at least some experience of management and/or leadership can construct a plausible discourse with only a superficial understanding of the subject. Or an author could have built an extremely successful career, and wanted to share their leadership insights with a wider audience. Whatever their motivation, the reader is left with the impression that what they are reading is valid and authentic, and therefore could be easily transferred into their own working life. Stop there!

If you're expecting the above from this second section, then you're going to be disappointed. The focus here is on how to discover the leadership qualities that will leverage Business Improvements, whatever level you're working at, whatever the nature of your work. Using the concept of the Russian Dolls, this book links a diverse range of topics (leadership, management, structured thinking, decision-making, recruitment and selection and succession planning) into an effective tool to deliver business improvements. Now this approach may seem obvious, but there are few texts that work in this way. Some specialize in particular areas of academic interest; some tell the story of how the author created (or is still creating) a wonderful business; some insist that their tools or approach are a sure-fire winner for any business. This book is different.

We'll start with your business opportunities, let you figure out how to realize the benefits of improving your business, and then encourage you get on with it. So the first Section ('Think Twice, Cut Once') introduces the 'Business Cube', Structured Thinking, Russian Dolls, and the Logical Levels Model. This second Section ('The Russian Dolls') links a clear tactical approach with the first Section. In a nutshell, first you understand your business, then implement improvements effectively and efficiently.

And there are some brief Case Studies at the end of the second Section that help you develop this reasoned approach to business improvements. There's no magic 'bullet' involved, no need for a superhuman effort to deliver business opportunities: just a rational and logical methodology to consistently delivering business improvements throughout your business.

Contents

Overview

These Sections have been developed around the 'Business Cube', which is shown below: it was introduced in Section 1.

For the moment, imagine that 'The Russian Dolls' are the heart of your business, and that the Cube is simply a construct, a clothes-peg, on which to hang a unifying business improvement theory. So think of the Cube in these terms: BC = RS(MS), where BC is the Business Cube, R = Resources, S = Standards, and (MS) is the Management System. Around this term, we define the these three components:-

Resources[3] -	*People, Parts* and *Process, Products* and *Services.*
Standards[4] -	*Quality* and *safety, Quantity* and *Time.*
Management Systems[5] -	*Forecast* and *Plan, Control, Report* and *Review*

The Business Cube:

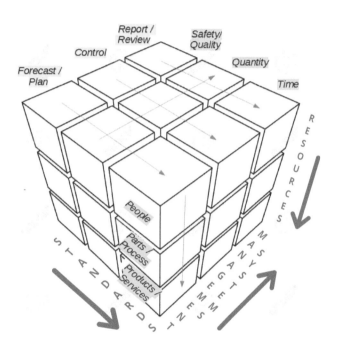

Inside the Business Cube, there are 3 Layers and 27 Blocks. And the focus here is with the top Layer, the 'People' Layer of Resources, that includes 9 Blocks. All these Blocks are engaged in the Leadership event - and for those of you who have read 'Think Twice, Cut Once', you'll notice that Leadership does not appear as one of the 29 tools. The reason is that it is far more important than a Tool. It is **business improvement critical**: there can be very little BI without a tangible Leadership input. Only once have I witnessed BI without Leadership, and that was when it happened by accident: 'we just accidentally improved the bottleneck process'.

So we use the Russian Dolls to emphasise some approaches to Leadership evaluation that may supersede the 'gut-feel', psychometric scores, and the 'How I Did It' thinking behind thousands of Leadership books. Rather like the Business Cube, these are approaches that were developed through extensive experience in BI projects, and the need to make the right 'leadership' decisions quickly and effectively.

Which means there has to be some Structured Thinking about Leadership - there has to be a structure that allows BI managers to make effective decisions about promoting leadership that can deliver business improvements. Not all leadership does this: in fact, most forms of leadership are geared towards maintaining the status quo, at whatever level of performance it happens to be.

To support your BI endeavours, we have a few original Tools available, and they can be used at any level. The Reward Triangle was mentioned in Section 1. And there are three difficult subjects that frequently confront BIs. Firstly, **decision-making**[6]: often the 'Cinderella' of any improvement. We use clear leadership and management processes and systems to streamline this. Then the **recruitment and selection**[7] of people at every level, starting with the No.1 Russian Doll (The Boss), and cascading through to the workforce. Consider this to be one of the basic elements of sustainable Business Improvement, closely followed by **succession planning**[8]. And that means at every level, starting with the No.5 Russian Dolls and working upwards to the No.1 Boss. There's a reason for reversing the sequence when comparing recruitment and selection against succession planning: this is discussed in the final Section 6, the **Business Cube - Processes and Systems.**

Looking at the diagram below **(Implementation Model)**, it links the Resources with Standards with Management Systems, including the Business Cube.

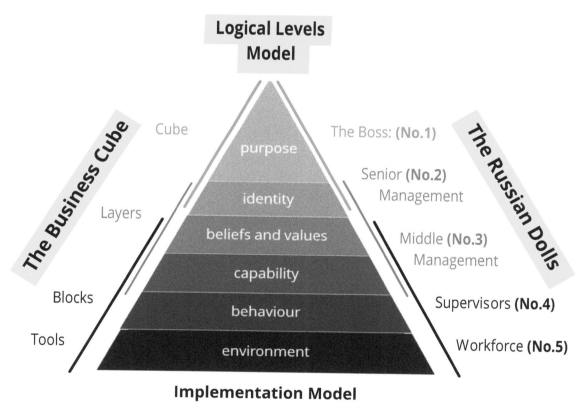

Implementation Model

The 'Tactical' implementation of business improvements is almost complete: this expands the content of Volume , and leaves the final Volume to focus on the Tools of BI, particularly the 'numbers' side of **BC = RS(MS)**. And numbers are the lifeblood of any business. So the final Section will bring together all three Volumes into one comprehensive BI trilogy.

So this Section will cover much of the same subject matter that recurs in many 'leadership' books: the twist is this material is framed within the Business Cube, which allows us to disentangle some of the confused thinking about leadership. So let's start now....!

1. The Russian Dolls

So where did the concept of the Russian Dolls in business improvement come from? As with many ideas in Section 1, 'Think Twice, Cut Once', it is my own invention - again created as a necessity. A necessity because any BI simply had to get done: as the cliché says, 'failure is not an option'[9]. And when it comes to investor's cash financing businesses, then success is paramount for them. So any BI manager has to think very clearly about the information needed to achieve any defined and agreed Improvement: and that means removing the information clutter that always surrounds these Improvements. And the first topic to remove is 'Organization'[10].

This will always be a fascinating subject for thousands of BI professionals - the sheer volume of work that can be generated, and PowerPoint slides created, seems endless. And you think your customers should pay for this? Of course! It's part of the cost-base that erodes your margins and can make your product/service less competitive. And, as a BI Manager, you automatically accept that the Organization chart (with Spans-of-Control[11], Skill's Matrices[12] etc.) will be one of the first documents to alight in your e-mail in-box. Which tells you something about the business priorities of most Human Resources Department.

True Story: When researching 'Organization', I discovered the website (https://www.iedunote.com) which provides a simple explanation of organization hierarchy.'3 levels of management in organizational hierarchy; (1) Top-level, (2) middle-level, (3) lower level. Top-level managers are responsible for setting organizational goals. Middle-level managers are engaged in carrying out their goals. Lower-level managers are responsible for running every work unit in an organization'. Please note that there are three levels, not five, as with the Russian Dolls. And note that the 'Boss' (No.1) level does not exist, as with the Workforce (No.5). So the two critical levels for effective BI are absent. This is one more reason why the subject of 'organization' is not developed further in this Volume, and why I try to avoid using the word altogether. Accompanying the article are three small sketches of managers representing the three different levels: all male, all white. And this is a 2020 publication!

The subject of 'organization' detracts from your BI focus: more importantly, it detracts from paying attention to 'Leadership'. If you think that an organization chart equates to a Leadership chart, then you are completely mistaken. And when was the last time your HR Department gave you a Leadership chart?

True Story: Some HR departments try to be helpful - they'll suggest placing a HR representative with the BI Team. This means that they can monitor you, the Team members and the BI. Just ask them for their updated Company Leadership chart and they'll forward their Organization chart with the title 'Organization' crossed out and replaced by the word 'Leadership'. Not even close!

The No.1 Russian Doll (The Boss) sits atop the Management structure: this person may or may not sit atop the leadership structure as well. So there's probably a division between the management and leadership teams with any BI initiative - and that applies if you are the owner, the manager, or whether it's a large or small business. Providing that the BI manager understands this then progress can be made.

To be clear, management is 'getting people to do what you want them to do': leadership is 'getting people to do what you want them to do and making them feel it's what they've always wanted to do'. Big difference, especially when being responsible for delivering a successful Business Improvement. And you will discover that you are 100% responsible for whatever happens.

Before discussing the Logical Levels Model and how it can work for the benefit of business improvement, let's examine 'responsibility' in the context of **authority, responsibility and accountability**[13] (ARA) and business improvement. Keeping it simple, **authority** is the ability to make binding decisions about your project's schedule, resources, activities, and products. **Responsibility** is the commitment to achieve specific results, and **accountability** is defined as bringing consequences to bear in response to people's performance. Time to check yourself and your BI Team against these criteria. Why? Because the **Standards** (Safety & Quality, Quantity, Time) you set for others are the ones that apply to yourself. So if there isn't a clear understanding within your BI Team, this weakness will be realised by others (often your peers) very quickly. So it's imperative to have an effective management operating system for yourself and your Team **before** even thinking about the action plan required for the BI.

To quote from the Projex[14] website, '*Remember, that **authority focuses on processes and responsibility focuses on outcomes**. Authority defines the decisions you can make but does not mention the results that you have to achieve, whereas responsibility addresses the results you must accomplish, but does not mention the decisions that you need to make in order to reach those results. From this it should be obvious that you can transfer the authority to make decisions to another individual, but that you cannot transfer the responsibility for the results of those decisions. As a final point, you can always take back authority that you gave to another individual, but you cannot blame the person for exercising their authority while they have it.* As can be inferred from the quote, the **alignment** of these three elements is absolutely critical for a successful BI: if one, or more, of these is misaligned, then there will be recurring problems, both within the BI Team, and with the wider group of participants. Nowadays, other tools have superseded the use of **ARA**, but the original is still a powerful method for understanding how the BI can succeed on a **tactical level**. When you're satisfied that they are aligned, then it's time to think about how to deploy the next Tool: the **Logical Levels Model**[15] (LLM).

This Model was developed in the 1970s., half a century ago: so it's tried and tested, but never fully exploited. Stemming from Neuro-Linguistic Programming (NLP)[15], which is a pseudo-scientific approach to communication, personal development, and psychotherapy, again developed in the 1970s., this pseudo-scientific approach can deter some BI managers, and that's regrettable. Because NLP and the LLM offer some elegant solutions to a few thorny issues that can undermine the success of your BI. More discussion in Section 2 about Structured Thinking, Leadership and the LLM.

Returning to the **Russian Dolls,** both the Management and Leadership Teams are capable of delivering the benefits - in theory. These Teams could be identical, though its unlikely, because from the smallest business to the biggest conglomerate, there's a shadow over every BI. That shadow is the counterpoint of every action that's taken to improve the business. I prefer to think of this influential group as the **Parrots**[16] - those beautiful birds that can mimic any human voice and management style! So the BI Manager has to be aware that there will be a relatively important group of managers who will be opposed to most BIs.

True Stories: One senior manager in a global corporation was so opposed to an Improvement Project that he stapled a copy of the legal contract between Client and Consultant on the Trade Union notice-board before the Project had even started.

Another assignment, another continent: the CEO was quietly opposed to the new owner's Improvement Project, so I recommended that he be made redundant. Never happened, but the new owner held this recommendation to ensure the CEO's full and unequivocal support. Pleased to say, he was highly co-operative.

The last example: Another senior executive decides to personally show me around the manufacturing facility. We walk across the road, enter the premises, start the tour, and he realises that we're touring the competitor's premises. Same industry with a look-alike process: so the No.1 Boss doesn't even know where his responsibilities are, literally!

These three examples are not uncommon. They represent the reaction of different groups to a BI, be they the management team, leadership team, 'parrots' or the owner's family, or even the BI Team itself. And they all need to be **aligned** with the BI goals. So **Step 1** is to understand who signed off on the Initiative, who authorized the investment, and who will be responsible and accountable for the results. Once you are satisfied that all aspects are correct, then move to the next key group, usually the Management Board or Executive Committee, and think of this as **Step 2.** Lock in place their agreement with the BI, and this is still at the Heads of Agreement level, before even thinking about a Work Plan for the BI.

This disciplined approach is essential for creating and securing the foundations of the BI, even with relatively small or seemingly trivial BIs. Short-cutting, or circumventing, these steps will undermine the BI at some point in the future. **Step 3** is to identify the senior managers who are directly involved with the BI: there will be other managers who may be indirectly involved, such HR., and their involvement has to follow after the 'direct' managers. Once this is agreement at the senior level, then the Work Plan (or Project Schedule) can be presented and discussed.

True Story: Signing off a Heads of Agreement for a Business Improvement may seem a formality: one top executive thought so, until the Sponsor decided that the same Improvement format being planned for one of his businesses could also be applied to another. In effect, this doubled the workload for the assignment, and meant that the Client received twice the potential benefits for the same financial outlay. The top executive signed off - and this can happen when you have the Authority without the Responsibility or Accountability for the end results.

The significance of the Russian Dolls is that they are all nested, stacked one inside the other: except for the Boss, who stands at the top, covering all other Dolls. And this arrangement means that the Boss's decisions should flow uninterrupted through the business structure: so any Improvement would simply be rolled out via the senior managers, middle managers and supervisors and to the Workforce. Very often, this does not happen, even with formal and informal incentives being brought to bear. So why not?

Two main reasons. Firstly, the Boss is lacking in some leadership skills that will have to be compensated for in the BI delivery: and secondly, the Senior Team are not automatically compensating for the Boss's deficiencies. Both these reasons reside with the Boss, who bears ultimate responsibility for the business, has the authority, and probably isn't holding themselves and/or the Senior Team accountable. And that Team do not believe it's their job, or within their ARA, to take corrective action. So call a group of professional BI managers to deliver the results, or read this book and figure out what to do next.

Step 4: Look in the **Management Mirror**[17], and here I quote from Joe Caruso's book. *'I find it fascinating that the overall attitude, productivity and level of customer service so consistently reflects the management style of a department, or even the entire organization'......'This management mirror theory has allowed me to correlate specific poor management styles with expected overall employee attitude and performance'.* For 'management' read leadership, because if it was just management, then systems and processes might contain the issues created. In the case of Leadership, the issues are magnified: why? *'Because your people will mimic you. This means: if you don't start your meetings on time, neither will your people. If you are painfully slow at making decisions, your people will be too. If you are defensive when you get negative feedback, don't expect your people to invite constructive criticism.* This is called the **'Law of Imitation'**[18] : in the simplest terms, it means to copy the action of others. And when linked with a collaborative organization structure - the Russian Dolls - then imitation becomes tremendously influential.

True Story: *Ever marvelled at how quickly human beings 'learn' when meeting their new boss for the first time: this is especially true when the Senior Team meet their new CEO, who has been appointed to radically improve business performance. Five minutes into their first Board Meeting, it's often difficult to recognize some Board Members from what they're now saying - it's as if they've had a 'business-brain transplant' in a matter of minutes.*

Step 5:   One would expect the next Step to be about middle management, Level 3. It's actually about Level 4, the Supervisors. This is because Supervisors are the third most important Level in any BI, after the Boss and Senior Management. This is the Level that actually gets things done, makes things happen, and one of the core functions of Levels 1 and 2 is to ensure that Level 3 is taking the 'right' actions. The term 'right' actions may seem vague, because the 'right' actions are not just defined in business terms, but also in ethical[19], environmental and legal[19] terms. Which comes to one of the key uses of the Business Cube. Because the whole business is captured within the Cube, then all other considerations are 'on the table' to be discussed - there are no considerations that are outside the business remit. This inclusiveness is critical - as you can read below.

True Story: *It made commercial sense to reduce expenditure on equipment maintenance for a Liquid Natural Gas Plant (LNG): in practical terms, that meant that some equipment was not maintained to the required mechanical standards, which led directly to a catastrophic failure.*
In another example, for business reasons, the processing of raw materials was placed within converted shipping containers. In terms of personal safety for employees, and compliance with electrical standards, then this manufacturing option should never have been considered, let alone implemented.

Business is conducted within an ethical, environmental and legal framework in any region or country. This scope has to be included in any business improvement, and in the decision making process. This requires active management, not a response in terms of passive management, which is often viewed as Management By Exception (MBE)[20].

Right between Senior Management and the Supervisory Level are the Middle Managers, Dolls No. 3, and this is where the Russian Dolls and Leadership become less clear. Taking the cascade of information coming from The Boss and Senior Team, the Middle Managers should be able to translate this into an effective Action Plan for Improvement with the help of the Supervisors. In very few instances does this actually happen.

This is what really happens. The Improvement strategy is announced, hopefully with a set of goals: it's signed off by the Senior Team, passed onto the Middle Managers, and then becomes part of their workload. At which point the Business Improvement might re-appear as something very different.

True Story: *In some meetings, you can count the number of times a middle manager agrees with the Improvement, accepts the need to deliver the benefits, then continues the sentence with the word 'but'....There then follows a list of very logical reasons why the Improvement may or may not happen. A quick tally of the 'buts' at the end of the meeting indicates the level of resistance: at worst, this can kill an Improvement, and, at best, it provides a filter where the improvement logic is critically assessed yet again.*

If this is the case, then the key to success is **Involvement.** That means getting Middle Managers physically and mentally working on the BI: physical where possible, and thinking about the BI whenever possible.

True Story: *In the early stages of one BI, the Improvement Team demonstrated that processing productivity could be doubled: the Middle Managers had some doubts, so we trained them in skills required for the new positions, and set them to work. Using Single Piece Flow[22], over a given time period, they doubled productivity, convincing themselves that the BI is a viable and profitable option.*

Involvement is inevitable for Supervisors and the Workforce (Doll No. 5). They have to engage, and the **quality** of that engagement is absolutely critical for success. By quality, I refer to the leadership aspect: there is a need to be completely knowledgeable of the requirements of the Business Improvements, the process and procedural changes, every aspect of the 'new way of working'. Remember that you have to lead by example and communicate the BI at every relevant opportunity: there are few second chances when it comes to reinforcing the credibility and viability of the Improvement.

So before starting to make the changes required, it's essential to complete a full check of everything. For this purpose, the Business Cube is excellent. This approach reduces the chances of forgetting something: it's similar to Failure Mode Evaluation Analysis (FMEA), only for Business Improvements, as it compels the BI Manager and Team to think through all aspects of the Improvement. More about this in Volume 3, where the Business Cube is developed further.

QUESTIONS - **RUSSIAN DOLLS and LEADERSHIP**

A few quick questions about Section 1:

Q1.   How many Dolls are there?   _____

Q2.   Which is the third Doll?   _____

Q3.   From a business improvement perspective, which are the three most important Dolls?
_____

Q4.   What is the 'Management Mirror'?   _____

Q5.   What is the 'Law of Imitation'?   _____

Q6.   What do the initials ARA stand for?   _____

SUMMARY: RUSSIAN DOLLS

1.   **Russian Dolls** are a way of aligning the Business organization with the Logical Levels - and this allows the BI Manager and Team to focus on the business drivers, the cost structure, and the business proposition for the customer. They downplay organization charts, spans-of-control, the influence of HR and other indirect activities. In essence, they allow us to focus on the customer.

2.   **Leadership** is an essential ingredient for effective Business Improvements. The Logical Levels act as the medium through which Business Improvements are delivered. That's because each Logical Level poses certain questions. So Supervisors are responsible for answering the 'What', 'Where' and 'When' questions posed by the Workforce, and so are the Workforce themselves. More about this in Sections 4 and 5.

3.   The Boss focuses on the 'What else' and 'Who' questions (the 'Purpose' and 'Identity'), particularly the 'Purpose'. If you think this is contrived, consider the possibilities of the Boss 'tweeting' every employee in the Workforce about the daily progress of any Business Improvement. Think about the impact that the former President of the United States, Donald Trump, had when this became a daily/weekly event. As a BI Manager, could you live with that on your assignment: I have experienced this leadership style, and it's not a beneficial experience!

4.   So this structure promotes clear thinking coupled with defined Leadership Levels : and remember that problems or opportunities at the 'Environment' level can only be fixed at the 'Behaviour' Level or above. Example: the lighting is too dim (Environment), you have to flick the 'on' light switch (Behaviour), and you may need training to know where the light switch is located (Capability).

2. Structured Thinking about Leadership - The Logical Levels Model

'A commitment to structured, clear thinking brings quality results that drive critical IT stability and produce real cost savings as we stop solving the same problems over and over and over again'. This is a quote from an article by Kepner Tregoe (Christoph Goldenstern, 2021), which promotes their approach to structured problem solving.

Now let's take this philosophy and extend it's scope - beyond IT stability and problem solving. Think about using a structured approach to managing and leading a business: this was one of the key points discussed in Section 1 ('Think Twice, Cut Once'), and the **'Implementation Model'** on Page 5 takes this concept to the next level.

If you're going to think about implementing BIs in your business using a structured approach, then there has to be a structure, and the Implementation Model provides this. This Model combines three distinct elements - the Business Cube (Section 1), the Russian Dolls and Leadership, and the Logical Levels Model (LLM). The LLM derives from Neuro-Linguistic Programming (NLP), and a brief explanation of the mechanics of this Model is necessary before proceeding further. At this point, I'll refer to an excellent website (https://mechanicsofwhy.com) that explains the LLM.

'Paradoxically this tool (LLM) is neither particularly logical nor based on levels, yet can be useful as an aid to our thinking about change, facilitating a change process, and in any significant coaching dialogue. In our own work we have found it helpful as a way of organising thinking about a problematic situation or unexploited opportunity, provided our overall approach is **systemic'** [21].

The original LLM was proposed by Robert Dilts in the 1980's and variations have since appeared under a range of titles, including "Neuro-logical Levels" and "Logical Levels of Change". In his original version, Dilts described the levels as a kind of ladder with each level rising to the one above it: Environment to Behaviour to Capability to Beliefs and Values to Identity to Purpose. Subsequently this became a pyramid with Environment at the bottom and Identity at the top, with Purpose at the top level. The Model shown below is courtesy of Dilts, and he termed it the Logical Levels of Change, with the six interrogative words aligned with the six levels.

Dilts: Logical Levels of Change

Albert Einstein referred to his own concept of logical levels thinking: *'The significant problems we face cannot be solved at the same level of thinking we were at when we created them'.* The implication being that we need to move up at least one logical level to solve our problems. Taking this approach, it's possible to describe the Model in a way that makes it appear to follow a logical sequence. And that's the beauty of this Model: *'to be useful as a way of deciding at what level of thinking a response needs to occur for the results to be sustainable over time. The general principle is to identify what level or levels the problem or opportunity occupies and to then recognise that if a particular intervention does not work, it is almost certain that the root cause will be at a higher (or deeper, depending on which way is 'up') logical level than the presenting symptom'.* To be concise, the following logic applies: *'The more I practice the right things, the better I get. The better I get, the more my confidence in my skill, and my consistency, increases. The more my consistency increases, the more I begin to believe in myself.* [22] **This is what we** (www.vievolve.com: www.telossolutions.co.uk:) **do when introducing our clients to it as a way of facilitating change, or as a way of beginning to turn a failing project around**[22]**'**

All these quoted sections reflect their *'strong preference for taking a **systemic approach** because, in their experience, that is what delivers the most successful and robust results in business'*. So the LLM is a key component of my Business Implementation Model: whereas **thinking systematically**[22] is the underlying approach for the Business Cube. Because the distinction between these two approaches is often blurred, I opted for the phrase **structured thinking** to encompass both approaches under one generic umbrella - an attempt to 'Keep It Simple'!

Clarity of the Business Improvement communication is critical for success: then Leadership from the Boss can have a unifying impact for all the Russian Dolls, and can permeate through the entire business. With structured thinking at the core of both the Cube and the Implementation Models, it becomes so much easier to **explain logically** why the business is going to deliver on a particular BI.

True Story - It's a simple exercise to take any manager through the LLM. Blu-tack six sheets of blank A0 (flip-chart) paper to a suitable wall, and write the titles of the each of the six levels at the top of each sheet, starting with 'Environment' on the far left, and working through to 'Purpose' on the far right. Then ask them to describe the environment where they work, and then when they work. So, for example, a night shift manager would describe his working environment and working hours. The same procedure follows for 'Behaviours' (what you do), and then 'Capabilities '(what skills you possess to action your behaviours at work). Normally, all goes well until the 'Values and Beliefs' Level is reached. By now, the manager has the measure of this exercise, and they start to talk about their Business Values, which can be a little difficult, and their Business Beliefs can become a real struggle, and then their Identity (who they are within the Business) is often a problem. This pattern of responses is seldom found in the Boss or Senior Managers, which is to be expected, and, surprisingly, in the Supervisory Level. So three out of the five Dolls are often aligned, with the Middle Manager Level the most prone to being out-of-step with the BI. For this exercise, the Workforce are sometimes involved, depending on the the BI requirements.

*The purpose of this exercise is to 'flush out' any Values and Beliefs that are simply misaligned, or non-existent, with the goals of the BI. For example, meet the 'Health and Safety Manager' who believes that their primary responsibility is to 'get along with people so that they can get their work done'. Seems plausible until you **think through** the implications of this approach when dealing with hazardous environments and working conditions. And this experience can be replicated in many businesses, and has to be addressed before the BI gets under-way.*

Looking at the Model below, the LLM sits at the apex of the Implementation Model. If you've already read Volume 1, then The Business Cube will known to you. What was not revealed was the Implementation Model, and how your **Business Understanding** comes from the Cube, which then

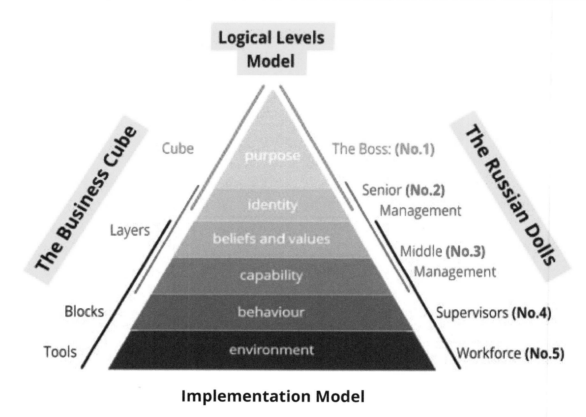

Implementation Model

feeds the data/information/knowledge into the **Implementation Model**. So the LLM is essentially the medium through which the BI is delivered: it's the oil that lubricates the BI to evolve successfully almost friction-free, bar a few disagreements along the way. This is my preferred way of working: why?

There are some simple answers to this question:-

1. Less mental 'wear-and-tear' for all parties and individuals when working consensually, towards an agreed Business Improvement goal.

2. Encourages both systematic and systemic thinking, what we have called **structured thinking**: which means that **logic** can prevail inside a defined structure (The Business Cube) for **understanding**, and inside a defined structure (The Implementation Model) for **getting the BI delivered** with a profitable outcome.

3. Takes the technical aspects of some BI work (which may be highly complex), and streamlines data/information/knowledge flows into **actionable** tasks. More about this in Volume 3, when we examine the Tools used to manage a successful BI.

4. Lastly, and stated openly without the intention of upsetting the reader, I prefer my BI Teams and everybody associated with the Improvement to be inside the tent pissing out, rather than outside the tent pissing in. Never think that this is an automatic given for any BI.

True Story: New assignment, new country and new Team: one of the key Team Members introduced himself by marching into the room, squaring up to me, and saying in a loud voice, 'You've got my project!'. He was definitely standing outside the tent!

Now let's turn to the Russian Dolls and Leadership. For those Senior Managers and the Boss to deliver a successful BI, there needs to be structured approach to Implementation. Too often have I witnessed a winning BI undermined by the careless comment, the throwaway aside, from a Manager not directly involved.

True Story: Having completed the first week of any Implementation, some managers will question the results, and that questioning will start with the Workforce and feed through to the Supervisory level. Instead of probing the results at a peer level, they try to challenge the validity of the entire effort.

The Implementation Model has three different coloured bars running between the LLM and the Russian Dolls: the **red** one (The Boss), stretching from 'Purpose' to 'Identity'. Those are the levels that the Boss needs to focus on when communicating the BI message. And that message has to be consistent and unequivocal. Then there's the **blue** line, that covers the levels from 'Identity through Beliefs and Values to Capabilities'. Senior and Middle Management need to identify with the BI to the same extent as the Boss: and that identification impacts their business beliefs and values about the need and potential benefits of delivering the BI. To achieve this commitment and involvement, each member of the Senior and Middle Team has to have the skills and capabilities to deliver their share of the necessary work. That means that they're experienced and qualified in their respective fields.

True Story: It's also a useful opportunity for the BI Manager to understand whether each Senior Manager is 'thinking at the right level'. Which can be critically important for the success of the BI. On one assignment in Europe with a large car component manufacturer, a new HR Director had been brought in from the United States to fill the senior HR role in that business. This person was outstandingly competent: so much so that I insisted that the senior manager on our BI Team meet him to appreciate what an excellent ally he could be for the Initiative: and he was.

Sometimes Middle Managers struggle with their roles, and this can be for a variety of personal or team issues. Dr. Alastair Mant in his book 'Leaders We Deserve', says it better than I can.

1. The boys at the top: *not necessarily very clever or very responsible, but at least safe enough to think about alternatives: rather isolated from consumer.....*

3. The people at the bottom of the organizations, *producers and consumers...many of whom care about the standards, quality and purpose of things....*

2. The risers in the middle, *focused on competition and movement rather than the verities of life, and perpetually threatened by the possibility of **1.** and **3.** talking to each other.....a few of them are really dangerous.*

And that sums up the tactical dilemma: there may be some Middle Managers who are essential for the success of the BI, and yet are wavering in their enthusiasm and support. Even if some of them decide to opt out of the BI Team for whatever reasons, the fact is that constant monitoring of their individual performance within the Team is necessary.

True Story: A small group of Senior and Middle Managers were responsible for the engineering quality of a piece of hi-tech equipment: with only 26 components in this piece, almost of the parts had been incorrectly designed, so the kit simply did not (and could not) work. This meant that the planned redundancies of some of these people had to be postponed, and it was back to the proverbial drawing board (or CAD/CAM) for a design that was not flawed.

This is not an isolated case: the simple fact is that these Russian Dolls need lots of attention, constantly. As a BI manager, you have to think through the consequences of taking time away from the assignment.

True Story: I took a scheduled one week holiday after the promised financial results had been achieved and signed off by the Client. Just before leaving home on the return trip, I received a phone call from my Boss asking me to go straight to the BI Team hotel, not the Client site. Apparently, one of the BI Team Members had agreed with the Client's HR Director to have me removed from the assignment. After the results had been agreed and signed off.

The moral of this story is clear: as a BI Manager, you have to be aware of what is going on around you, even when you're not there. And the only good news from the above story is that the BI Team Member was not the one I left in charge during my absence, so my holiday timing might have been suspect, but my judgement of an individual's character was spot-on.

And lastly, there's the **'black'** line that runs from 'Beliefs and Values through to Environment'. This impacts Doll Nos. 4 and 5, the Supervisors and Workforce. These two Dolls are critical to the success or failure of the BI: and that means you have to be clear about the BI message, the use of structured thinking about how to roll out the Improvement, and using the LLM to understand any BI issues, and then what action is going to be taken to address those issues.

These three coloured lines mark the five Russian Dolls to the six Logical Levels: they clarify the message and content that should be delivered by the each level of Dolls. So if your a Supervisor on Level 4, then make sure you can answer the 'What' questions (Behaviour), and the 'Where and When' (Environment) questions that will be coming from your Team, the Workforce (Level 5). And when you are answering questions from your Team, and those questions start with 'Why', then have a Manager present. By now, I hope you're beginning to understand the power of the LLM to clarify the Implementation Model. So how does the Business Cube (the other side of the triangle) fit with the LLM and the Russian Dolls?

From Volume 1, we've learnt that the Cube presents all the relevant data/information/knowledge via a structured approach that comes from **structured thinking**. So the contents of the entire Cube (all 27 Blocks and 3 Layers) are available to The Boss and Senior Management Team. Being available does not mean that it is used, or that any interest is even shown in the content: but it's there. Cut to the next Level, Layers, and you can see that it impacts the 'Identity', 'Beliefs and Values' and 'Capabilities' of the LLM. That's exactly what happens with the 'People' Layer: they should receive and communicate all the Content that's required to deliver the BI in the most effective and efficient manner. This is where many 'indirect' Departments (such as HR, Legal, Accounts) come into play. And please remember that the Layers include 'Parts/Process' and 'Products/Services', which can involve automation and other developments. For the purposes of Business Improvements and the Implementation Model, it's 'People' that are the key to success. Which leads into the next two Section headings: 'Leadership levels' and 'Decision-making'.

Before proceeding further, let's help you find out your understanding so far: a few simple questions to think about and answer:-

QUESTIONS - **STRUCTURED THINKING about LEADERSHIP** - The Logical Levels Model

A few quick questions about Section 2:

Q1.　How many Logical Levels are there?　_____

Q2.　Which Logical Level sits at the bottom of the Triangle?　_____

Q3.　Which Doll occupies the the most important Level when it comes to business improvement?　_____

Q4.　The Business Cube has how many Cubes?　_____

Q5.　How many Blocks are there in the Cube?　_____

Q6.　Why are the Workforce (Doll No.5) included in the Implementation Model?　_____
_____

SUMMARY - STRUCTURED THINKING about LEADERSHIP - The Logical Levels Model

1.　**Structured thinking** are a viable approach with the Business Cube - it provides a logical format for understanding the key data/information/knowledge for your business.

2.　**The Logical Levels Model** is derived from neuro-linguistic programming. There are six Levels in the Model, and they act as the medium through which Business Improvements are delivered. That's because each Level poses certain questions for the five Russian Dolls.

3.　The Boss focuses on the 'What else' and 'Who', the Purpose and Identity, particularly the 'Purpose'. if you believe this is contrived, consider the possibilities of the Boss 'tweeting' every employee in the Business about the daily progress of any Business Improvement. Think about the impact that the former President of the United States, Donald Trump, had when this became a daily/weekly event. As a BI Manager, could you live with that on your assignment: and I have experienced this leadership style.

4.　From the diagrams shown in this Section, it's clear that certain Russian Dolls become responsible for LLM levels - for example, Supervisors are responsible for answering the 'What', 'Where' and 'When' questions.

5.　So this promotes clear thinking coupled with defined leadership: and remember that problems or opportunities at the 'Environment' level can only be fixed at the 'Behaviour' Level or above. The lighting is too dim (Environment), you have to flick the 'on' light switch (Behaviour), and you may need training to know where the light switch is located (Capability).

3. Leadership Levels

Access the Internet and type in amazon.co.uk : then, in the 'Search' box on their website, type in 'Leadership Books', and the following statement appears:-

1-16 of over 100,000 results for "leadership books"

The first 16 listed titles that discuss Leadership appear on the screen: and that's the first 16 of the first 100,000 books. Leadership is one of the most over described attributes of a successful BI. Which means that this subject still needs to be covered, and the coverage has to be laser focused on the requirements of a business improvement. So every effort has been made to be succinct and direct. Yet it's still a slippery subject to discuss. And because of the Section title, 'Leadership Levels', it is not a copy-over of John Maxwell's well-known book 'The 5 Levels of Leadership: Proven Steps to maximize your Leadership' (2011). Our Levels are linked to the Russian Dolls.

The Russian Dolls have to provide effective leadership at every Level, and not just for those Team Members who are subordinate to them in the business organization chart or hierarchy. Before you can lead others, you have to learn to lead yourself. And leading yourself can be problematic at any Level. Take the the No.1 Boss. They have to demonstrate, and be seen to demonstrate, a command of the 'Purpose' and 'Identity' of the BI: which means that they've assessed the alternative actions that could be taken, and decided to start this particular BI. They have also decided who will be involved, both directly and indirectly, in leading and managing the BI. These two activities are essential, but don't think that they will happen automatically.

True Story: I remember starting a BI having not met the Boss, nor the Senior Managers who had been assigned to lead and manage it, with just a remit to 'fix the business problem'. The BI analysis was wafer-thin, so it was an very interesting first few weeks of work.

Now there might be some readers who would expect the Boss to roll-up their shirt sleeves and get stuck in: that's not required or necessary. The adage 'don't buy a dog and start barking yourself' applies here. Or they might expect the Boss to hold all the 'Beliefs and Values' to make the BI a success: not necessary. I expect the Senior and Middle Managers to have those Beliefs and Values in the BI. I expect the Boss to be professionally sceptical of the BI throughout it's life-cycle. There has to be a continuously critical assessment of the business merits of the Improvement: and it's one of the Boss's jobs to provide that assessment. The Boss must never fall in love with the BI: they just need to be in love with their customers.

Let's be clear: the Boss handles 'Identity' and 'Purpose' of the BI. Now the Senior Managers focus on 'Identity', 'Beliefs and Values', and 'Capability'. There's an obvious overlap here, and that's important. They have to ensure that all the Team Members have the skills to do their jobs, and are aligned with the BI goals. And at their Level, they need to demonstrate some leadership qualities, by setting agreed standards and behaviours and practising those standards and behaviours at all times. Remember the adage, 'Monkey see, monkey do': your Team Members will learn and imitate your behaviours very quickly. And this also sets the pace for the Middle Managers - this is the Level that sometimes has doubts about the 'Why' of the BI - so they need to focus strongly on the 'How', and the 'Capabilities' of their Team Members to deliver the BI within all agreed parameters.

True Story: Spent a few hours studying the efficiency of a bottle-neck machine changeover on a production line, and I noticed that several vital minutes were being lost on every changeover. I reviewed the findings with the Middle Manager responsible, and he became annoyed - not with me, but with his Supervisors. 'They should have spotted this', he says. True, and the Manager should have checked their capability to spot this: they were all Supervisors who were dedicated engineers by profession.

So the Dolls are demonstrating leadership, and that leadership is **different** for each Level. Yet there are always two common denominators in every form of that leadership: 'set the example' and 'communicate, communicate and communicate the BI message'. Whatever role you're playing in the BI, you will be a paragon of that role - whether you're the Boss or Manager or just an outside contractor. And you will 'talk with people' about the BI, every aspect of the BI that you are knowledgeable about, and encourage others to do the same. So setting the example and communicating becomes the behavioural norm for Bosses and Managers - which means that they are able to 'lead by example'.

And leading by example is another management cliché that is frequently deployed in autobiographical books by famous business people. Understand exactly which behaviours need to be adopted by BI Team Members, and by people in different Levels: and which behaviours need to be downplayed. So constant questioning of the viability of the BI is excellent at the Boss level, but tedious at the Middle Management Level. Put simply, it's not part of the Middle Manager's remit to constantly question, and this scenario usually ends with the Manager being told to be quiet, which is not a very satisfactory response. So use the Implementation Model to explain logically why this is not the preferred example to set: because as soon as the Manager questions the viability, the Supervisory and Workforce start to question. It's the cascade of behaviours that the Russian Dolls represent: the way opinions can erode hard data and observed facts.

The two groups who are always dealing with the reality of the improvements are Supervisors and the Workforce: they have to, unless they decide to leave the business. So much of the effort in terms of discussion, re-training and personal/team development will focus on them. and especially the Supervisors. A whole industry has been created that focuses on personal and team development, what are termed the 'soft' or 'tactical' skills, the 'people' skills, needed to get the job done. And those skills often start at the individual level, aimed at improving the person, with the consequence that the Team, and therefore your business, will ultimately benefit. Possibly, but often not the case. Better to understand from the Middle Manager Level, through 'Capability', exactly what training is required, both in technical and tactical terms.

True Story: Some BIs are large in terms of capital spend, business impact, number of people involved. And some have a very tight time constraint: they absolutely have to get done within a narrow time-frame. I developed a system of 'Pyramid' training[23] (not the Pyramid physical fitness training!) to increase involvement of the Supervisory and Workforce levels in the delivery of effective training, and reduce the workload on myself. Be happy to share this with any interested parties.

Once the Training Needs Analysis has been completed, then develop the Supervisors to deliver the material, unless it's highly technical or specialist. And build any new materials into the standard training pack, ensuring that there are up-to-date and relevant. More about this in Volume 3, The Business Cube.

So every Leadership Level is addressing a specific narrative in terms of answering critical questions. And that narrative has to be **structured**: that means planned, prepared, and not off-the-

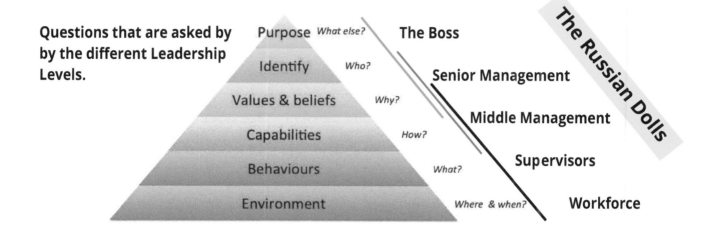

Questions that are asked by by the different Leadership Levels.

Purpose *What else?* — The Boss

Identify *Who?* — Senior Management

Values & beliefs *Why?* — Middle Management

Capabilities *How?*

Behaviours *What?* — Supervisors

Environment *Where & when?* — Workforce

The Russian Dolls

cuff. Which means that thought has be given to exactly **what** you want the Supervisors and Workforce to do differently. And I mean exactly!

Smart Bosses will ask the BI Manager what they want them to do before kicking off the Improvement: the BI Manager has to be ready with a clear answer. The same logic applies to both the Senior and Middle Managers - questions about 'Who', 'Why' and 'How' regarding the Business Improvement are their responsibility to answer. Too often I've witnessed Supervisors struggling to answer questions outside of their remit, legitimate questions posed by Workforce members. Remember that Supervisors are primarily addressing the 'What', 'Where' and 'When', and not so much the 'Why' and 'How'.

True Story: We're halfway through a business 'Commitment' meeting, where the whole Company agrees to deliver the agreed Production Plan for the coming week. In walks the Managing Director, and the whole ambience of the meeting changes in a second. Managers leaning against the wall are suddenly standing upright: questions become more incisive. He only stayed for 10 minutes, but the informal message was clear. The MD thinks that this meeting is sufficiently important to warrant a personal visit: and this was in a large food processing company.

When was the last time your Boss attended a meeting that promoted a BI that you were leading? Can't recall: have you tried asking them to attend? Probably not, because the downside could be a BI disaster.

True Story: My Boss was overseeing a BI launch for a project that was only a few miles away from where I was managing another Improvement. For some reason, the Head of the Consulting Company decided to attend that other BI launch. Oh dear! The meeting went very badly, the Head was very unhappy, and I escaped! The reason for the poor meeting: a lack of preparation with the Middle Managers.

To be clear: no matter what the Leadership Level, preparation is key. There is no other way. Never make assumptions about anything, whether they're technical or tactical: question everything until the logic is bullet-proofed and you, as the BI Manager, are satisfied. Accept nothing less!

So what does acceptable mean? This is a word that achieves for Business Improvement what the word reasonable does for English Law. It allows a flexible interpretation of the prevailing standards. In terms of Business Improvement, this can be dangerous. Take the recent disaster at Grenfell Tower[24], now a derelict 24-storey residential tower block in North Kensington, London, the remains of which are still standing following a severe fire in June 2017. Classed as an upgrade to reduce energy consumption for individual apartments, one of the fundamental flaws was a lack of agreement over the standard of materials used for external cladding. An example of technical standards being compromised.

Yet there are clear standards for the delivery of Business Improvements. Take the City Guilds 'Business Improvement Techniques' (7576), providing all of the skills (from basic to advanced) in order to effectively monitor and make improvements to production and manufacturing processes. There is assessment in the workplace and on completion of this qualification, and this is across a variety of business improvement roles. Or the Skills Training UK (2019 Training provider Winner of the Year) 'Business Improvement Techniques', with workplace related projected *identifying and tackling three workplace related projects on Quality, Cost and Delivery.* That's before the numerous Degrees in a range of subjects from *Foundation Degree Business Improvement Techniques* (West Nottinghamshire College) to a *Msc. in Business Improvement* (Ulster University), or perhaps *The Art and Practice of Systems Thinking,* an on-line Course from Harvard Business School.

Whatever your needs or preferences, there are professional bodies that can deliver expert tuition in Business Improvement across all industries. If this is the case, then the knowledge is available, but the Improvement results are still falling short of planned outcomes. Why?

Our contention is that there are **weaknesses in the deployment model** for many planned Business Improvements: and the weakness starts at the Boss Level (No.1). Most Bosses have never been BI Managers, or Project Managers aiming to improve business performance: they may have been BI Team Members at some point in their career development, so have an understanding of what's involved. Now, they are the Boss: they have to set the example and lead the way for their business, and it's logical to assume that the same business approach that took them to the top in their Company is going to work for Business Improvements. Not true.

Effective Bosses understand that their involvement is most beneficial at **the Front-End** of any BI (check the Infrastructure and Projects Authority (IPA) website (https://www.gov.uk/government/organisations/infrastructure-and-projects-authority) definition of the Front End), which involved the setting up of the BI. From my experience, **most BIs fail because they were fundamental flaws in the design and planning of the Improvement from the very beginning.** That occurs because very few BI Managers have the guts to stand up to the Boss, and tell the Boss that their preferred approach is somewhat lacking. Occasionally, there's a need to practise 'Confrontation Management'.

True Story: I've only had one Boss tell me after a key meeting that he wanted to punch me out. The important point here is to always smile when you're telling them: it's difficult to punch somebody when they're smiling at you.

The second weakness is a BI Manager who often has the technical ability, but is lacking the personal skills to address business issues stemming from the proposed Improvement. There has to be a quality of independent thinking for any BI to succeed. If there's a Boss who is too overbearing, coupled with a BI manager who is reluctant to address BI issues, then it can be a recipe for failure. In some cases, that failure can be very expensive for everybody.

True Story: There's one film that is often mentioned for demonstrating Leadership qualities in the face of daunting odds, and that's *'Twelve O'clock High'* (1949). Another film that demonstrates a few performance improvement techniques for struggling Teams is *'The Brighton Miracle'* (2019), released some 70 years later. This film focuses on the Japanese rugby union football team struggling to win International matches: it's a master-class in how to improve team performance, though not for the faint-hearted. See if you can spot the 'Management Mirror' moment.
(https://www.thebrightonmiracle.com)

It's not by chance that businesses sometimes manage their Improvements in this way. And this third underlying weakness is repeatedly flagged up in the film: let's call it **the need to 'fit' in.** Officially, it's called the **psychology of conformity**, and it's a very powerful factor in BI Team dynamics, and the relationship that the BI Team has with the Leadership Levels, particularly the Boss. *Conformity means to change behaviours in order to fit in with the people around you. We want to be unique, but we want to fit in? And, what exactly is it we are all trying to fit in to?*

In business improvement terms, that should be the goals of the Improvement: in reality, that clarity can become blurred. Watching *'The Brighton Miracle'* film, there's a constant tug-of-war between those members of Japanese senior management who are worried that the new Coach does not 'fit' in with their current way of training, and the Rugby Coach (or Improvement Manager), who is focussed on winning their next major international rugby match. To paraphrase the character Yoda from the 'Star Wars' films, 'The forces of conformity, they can be strong'. Indeed they can, and often overwhelming. So resisting this inertia is essential.

With many businesses, how strong this resistance to change is has been built up over a period of years. And there are dozens of psychometrics that can be deployed to measure this resistance. When you're faced with the need to suddenly and dramatically improve business performance, then using psychometrics is technically correct and tactically wrong. My experience is to use something more rough and ready, yet just as indicative.

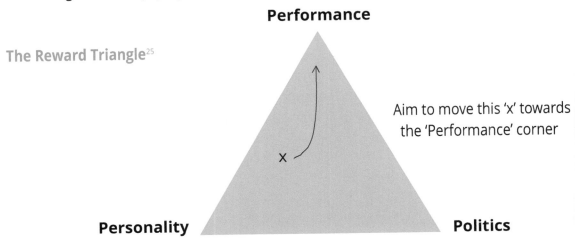

The Reward Triangle[25]

'What behaviours are you rewarded for? Are those behaviours based on Performance, Politics or Personality?' Whenever I've posed these questions to both Supervisory and Middle Management

Teams, the response has always leaned towards Politics or Personality. In other words, there's an aversion to Business Performance. This is a significant factor in understanding the **Reward System** that actually operates in all businesses. If the individuals and groups are not being rewarded for behaviour that drives improved business performance, then that is a sea-anchor on Business Improvements. That's a challenge for the BI manager, because the BI Team Members will normally be pulled from the same pool of candidates, so they automatically bring this 'working mentality' with them.

True Story: Using a different approach, I posed this question to the Boss and his Senior Management Team during a Training and Development Workshop. 'Do relationships build results, or results build relationships?' In terms of BI success, this is an important question: the responses reflected the reasons why the BI initiative had been started in the first place.

Leadership Levels clarify the role that each Level has to play in a successful BI - the questions will come from the first word. So a question that begins with 'What.....', is definitely at the Supervisory Level. If the Supervisor is unable to answer that question, then a Middle Manager steps in. After resolving the answer, then this Level need to understand 'How' they are going to avoid a similar issue happening again.

True Story: This may seem pedantic, but this discipline (or rigour) has to be applied to all BIs. Working in this way often forces the Middle Managers to confront issues that they may have been avoiding: and **avoidance** is one of the key reasons for many performance shortfalls in a business. This is a by-product of conformity - the unspoken need not to ask the awkward question. A large European car component manufacturing plant was the epitome of the unspoken question, the need to agree with the local management team, and the need to break that chain of command that defied Business Improvement.

QUESTIONS - **LEADERSHIP LEVELS**

A few quick questions about Section 3:

Q1.   How many Leadership Levels are there?   _____

Q2.   What is the No.5 Russian Doll called?   _____

Q3.   Which three letter word is used to describe the psychology of conformity?   _____

Q4.   What are the three elements in the Reward Triangle?   _____

Q5.   For the purposes of a BI, which element is the most important?   _____

Q6.   Why are there interrogative words associated with each of the six Logical Levels Model and the five Leadership levels?

_____

SUMMARY:

1.   **Leadership Levels** are portrayed as Russian Dolls - and there are five different Russian Dolls, each nested inside each other, with the Boss as No.1 Doll, the largest of the five.

2.   The behaviour of the Dolls at all Levels is critical for the success of any BI: they need to understand the questions they should be asking at each Level, thereby 'setting the example' and 'communicating' a consistent and useful message about the BI.

3.   The Leadership Levels take the data/information/knowledge gathered from the Business Cube and use the Logical Levels Model to guide their behaviours at every stage of the BI. By doing this, the BI Manager and Team can focus on the actions required to deliver the benefits of the Improvement.

4. Decision-Making

If the Logical Levels Model provides the oil to lubricate the Business Improvement process, then making decisions are the spark plugs. Skip this Section if you drive an electric vehicle. Only joking!

For the Implementation Model to work effectively, the right decisions have to be made at the right time by the right people: and that's the conundrum. Trying to resolve the indecision about how to make effective decisions, there are thousands of books, videos, pod-casts and multi-media events to promote an array of different approaches. This Section concentrates on some tried-and-tested 'Best Practice' approaches, and introduces them in the context of the Business Cube.

But the Business Cube is a separate entity to the Implementation Model, where most of the decisions are being made. So why start with the Cube? Because the first priority in all decision-making is to **understand** what is being decided. Then **understand** the consequences of making that decision. And the Cube is ideally suited to understanding the whole business, so let's use the same approach, and then carry on to think through the consequences of that decision. we use **structured thinking**, in the context of the Cube, to develop a **decision-making process**: and continue with the Cube approach to define the consequences of that decision. Here's a reminder of the Cube format:-

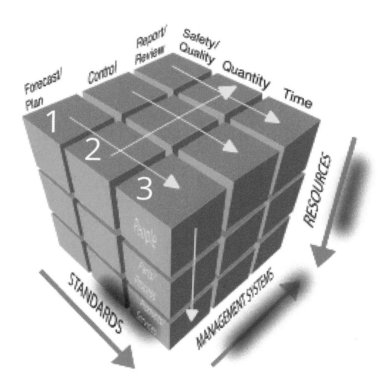

When you're making a business decision, understand where that decision is in the Cube. Is it at the 'Parts/Process' Level, or perhaps 'Products/Services'? Identify the Layer, then the Block: if you're deciding whether to install an improved Management Reporting System, look at Block 16 ('Parts/Process', 'Safety/Quality', 'Report/Review'), then start from Block 1 and think through the consequences of any changes. Many of these systems are now computerized, linked with other reporting systems, so if you change just one element it has an impact on other reporting systems.

All that's happening at the moment is that data/information/knowledge is being gathered: there's no decision in sight right now. So determine the facts before deciding.

This is where the Cube approach adds to the decision-making process: it provides the structure and allows structural thinking about the business. So the 'preparing' stage (Krogerus & Tschäppeler, TEDx, 2020), or 'checking the basics' phase (Matthew Confer, TEDx, 2012), can be done using a logical methodology. This approach has more likelihood of extracting accurate business details on which to base your decisions - it discourages the problem of 'garbage in / garbage out', often linked to software systems and databases. But there's no reason why this behaviour is limited to IT.

True Story: Joining an Improvement Project after nearly 7 weeks had elapsed, we had only 3 weeks to put together a detailed roadmap of Implementation for part of a large logistics business. Using the Cube approach, we completed the task with only a couple of days to spare: which was quite an achievement, given that the other Business Groups had been allowed over twice the time. The Cube approach helps to focus the mind on the important business facts, and link them together as a cohesive whole.

True Story: At exactly 8.00am every weekday morning, the Operations Manager began the daily update meeting. It was a PowerPoint show describing the previous day's performance, given by the Day manager. Everything went well, until one of the slides showed a number that was clearly incorrect: the Operations Manager's comment: 'Can't we trust the numbers any longer'?

Before making decisions, check the numbers: **always check the numbers.**

True Story: The Boss had decided to use a management operating system that allowed a generous interpretation of the business's performance: that was not understood by all managers, and there was a lengthy debate about the Reporting methodology. A poor quality decision, taken independently by the Boss, had consequences that cascaded through the business.

That decision could have been flagged up if the Business Cube had been used, or possibly if the decision had been taken by the Boss and the Senior Managers together.   Once the decision had been made, only a smart statistician working on the Implementation actions spotted the numerical anomaly. Over time, the significance of the anomaly faded in mathematical terms, but I hope somebody learned a lesson.

So you've got accurate data! Remember it has to be consistently accurate! Now the easiest part of decision-making: understanding exactly what you are deciding. Whether it's a decision taken by an individual, at whatever Level of the Russian Doll, or a group decision, about any subject, from business strategy to minor adjustments for routine procedures, there has to be thought given to both the decision and its potential consequences. This is what Matthew Confer describes as a 'Pre-Mortem' in his TEDx 2012 presentation.

True Story: A well-known firm of management consultants had developed a Production Planning System for one of their Clients. The software programme worked well, but had one software glitch. It progressively under-estimated the amount of product required by customers, so what actually looked like 'Lean' manufacturing was really anorexic for the business. A simple paper and pencil graph of future demand and current production would have shown this: but nobody checked the quality of automatic decisions being made about the raw material orders. Moral of the story: always check the output using a basic business sense approach. **Do the decisions look right?**

'Pre-Mortems' examine the potential consequences of a decision before that decision is made. Seems logical, but seldom done. Even with complex decisions involving multiple factors, this is rare. Because there's an innate preference for what I call **'Decision Lite'**. Those are decisions that are taken whilst on auto-pilot, at any level, including the BI Manager and Team. It's founded in taking complex issues and simplifying them, usually supported by a PowerPoint presentation. The diagram opposite shows the Eisenhower Matrix[26], and is not difficult to understand. And there are dozens of Decision Matrices available in the commercial marketplace. Whichever one you choose, or even if you create your own matrix for making business decisions, remember to 'check the basics' and avoid the 'decision lite' option. Get accurate data/information/ knowledge, develop a decision-making process that generates the 'right' decisions consistently for your business.

THE EISENHOWER MATRIX

Or doesn't keep generating the 'wrong' decisions! This is as, if not more, important than the 'right' decisions. Like the Business Cube, why do think that a two-dimensional Matrix is the answer to so many business issues? Because it's simple and easier for the manager to understand - so you persuade more potential customers (that's managers) to buy into it, then buy it and download it off the internet. There's a difference between easy and elegant: Watson and Crick's double helix model for DNA (remembering Rosalind Franks and Wilkins here) is elegant, but not easy: so all the Matrices I've ever seen have been easy but not elegant. The Decision Cube has a different approach.

The Decision Cube[27]

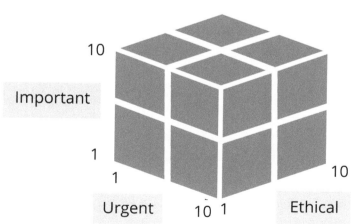

Imagine the same 'Important' and 'Urgent' dimensions as before, and then add an 'Ethical' element. This creates a more balanced assessment of the quality of decision-making. Easy to assess as well: score from 1 to 10 (1 is always the lowest) for the importance of the decision: then 1 to 10 for the urgency, and lastly 1 to 10 for the ethics of the decision. Now the word 'Ethics' can be replaced by 'Environment', and the same logic still applies. Once the three sets of scores are recorded, turn the total into a percentage. So '8 (Importance) + 8 (Urgency) + 3 (Ethical) = 19 / 30 = 63%. Glancing at the scores, this is a decision that has to be made, but there are some ethical issues that need to be addressed before proceeding. And it's possible to compare the overall score of different decisions, just to see whether there's a trend.

Story: Without naming names, I've witnessed some decisions that have been breathtakingly stupid. If a poor decision **can** be made, then, at some point, it will. And it could be very expensive for your business. Please don't think there's safety in numbers: teams are as likely to make poor decisions as individuals. Just look at Boeing's decision to continue with the MCAS upgrade on the 737 MAX. So to improve your business's performance in decision-making, make them **think through** the potential consequences of their actions (Pre-Mortem), making sure that the data is relevant and accurate (**Business Cube**), then install a **Decision Cube**. Recommended for Senior/Middle Managers, and even the Supervisory Level.

Perfect decisions do not exist, except in your own mind. So avoiding 'bad' decisions is as important as making 'good' decisions - although the difference between 'good' and 'bad' is highly subjective, it's surprising how participants instinctively understand the quality of decision-making. More structured thinking based on accurate data is the first way to improve. The second way is to simplify the structure of the management decision-making hierarchy. Which is where the Russian Dolls concept comes to the fore: and allowing each Doll Level to focus specifically on certain questions. Questions that start with 'What', 'Where' and 'When' are definitely the responsibility of Supervisors. The same logic applies for the other Dolls, which raises a critical point.

All too often, both Senior and Middle Managers tend to think at the wrong level. By that, they tend to think down - so Middle Managers focus on 'What', 'Where' and 'When', and they should be focusing on 'How'. This tendency can create real business problems, because it allows gaps in thinking to appear in the Business Improvement process. These gaps turn into business surprises because nobody was actually thinking about them.

True Story: The reverse can also be true. One Head of Human Resources in a major multi-national corporation was way above in his thinking. The HR plans for recruitment and selection, personal development and alignment with future business growth were all ahead of schedule. This is rarely the case.

Thinking at the 'wrong' level is all too common. The Implementation Model is a succinct way of re-aligning their thinking through a understandable structure. You can take them through the Logical levels Model, but it's often unnecessary: just quietly position their thinking.

Now there are two significant changes to decision-making: using the Business Cube, and then the Decision Matrix. In other words, improve the data/information/knowledge going into making the decisions, and then integrate an 'ethical' dimension into the process. Let's look at some examples where decision-making has been critical.

Take this decision: '*In 1977, the senior execs at 20th Century Fox made an astonishingly short-sighted decision. They signed over all product merchandising rights for any and all Star Wars films to George Lucas - in exchange for a mere $20,000 cut in Lucas' studio paycheck. The combined revenue from merchandising is estimated to have exceeded three billion dollars, and continues to grow annually, making it the most lucrative deal ever struck between an individual and a corporate studio in entertainment history. (Courtesy of Dr. Ilona Jerabek, from an article on her website, and re-printed in Forbes magazine by Erika Andersen, Oct.2013)'*. Clearly a matter of using the Business Cube to understand all the factors in play.

Or take these decisions: **'*Fatal flaw in Boeing 737 Max traceable to one key late decision*': Test pilots, engineers and regulators left in the dark about changes to MCAS system that would play a role in** two deadly crashes. Boeing continued to defend MCAS and its reliance on a single sensor after a first crash involving Indonesia's Lion Air. Four months later a second 737 Max crashed in Ethiopia. Within days the Max was grounded around the world.

The fatal flaws with Boeing's 737 Max can be traced to a breakdown late in the aircraft's development when test pilots, engineers and regulators were left in the dark about a fundamental overhaul to an automated system that would ultimately play a role in two deadly crashes. A year before the plane was finished Boeing made the system more aggressive and riskier. While the original version relied on data from at least two types of sensors, the ultimate used just one, leaving the system without a critical safeguard. In both doomed flights pilots struggled as a single damaged sensor sent the aircraft into irrecoverable nose-dives within minutes.

But many people involved in building, testing and approving the system, known as MCAS, said they had not fully understood the changes. Current and former employees at Boeing and the Federal Aviation Administration who spoke with the New York Times said **they had assumed** the system relied on more sensors and would rarely, if ever, activate.

Based on those **misguided assumptions**, many made **critical decisions affecting design, certification and training.** "It doesn't make any sense," said a former test pilot who worked on the Max. "I wish I had the full story."

While prosecutors and law-makers try to piece together what went wrong, the current and former employees point to the **single, fateful decision to change the system** which led to a series of design mistakes and regulatory oversights. As Boeing rushed to get the aircraft done, many of the employees described a **compartmentalised approach,** each focusing on a small part of the plane. The process left them without a complete view of a critical and ultimately dangerous system.

The company also played down the scope of the system to regulators. **Boeing never disclosed** the revamp of MCAS to FAA officials involved in determining pilot training needs, according to three agency officials. As a result most Max pilots did not know about the software until after the first crash in October. "Boeing has no higher priority than the safety of the flying public," a company spokesman, Gordon Johndroe, said in a statement. "The FAA considered the final configuration and operating parameters of MCAS during Max certification, and concluded that it met all certification and regulatory requirements."

At first MCAS – Manoeuvring Characteristics Augmentation System – wasn't a very risky piece of software. The system would trigger only in rare conditions, nudging down the nose of the aircraft to make the Max handle more smoothly during high-speed moves. And it relied on data from multiple sensors measuring the plane's acceleration and its angle to the wind, helping to ensure that the software didn't activate erroneously.

Then Boeing engineers re-conceived the system, expanding its role to avoid stalls in all types of situations. They allowed the software to operate throughout much more of the flight. They enabled it to aggressively push down the nose of the plane. And they used only data about the plane's angle, removing some of the safeguards. A test pilot who originally advocated for the expansion of the system didn't understand how the changes affected its safety. Safety analysts said they would have acted differently if they had known it used just one sensor. Regulators didn't conduct a formal safety assessment of the new version of MCAS.

The current and former employees, many of whom spoke on the condition of anonymity, said that after the first crash they were stunned to discover MCAS relied on a single sensor.

"It seems like somebody didn't understand what they were doing," said an engineer who assessed the system's sensors. (Courtesy of the Irish Times, June, 2019, Jack Nicas, Natalie Kitroeff, David Gelles, James Glanz).

I seldom reprint an article in almost its entirety: sometimes it's necessary. Every decision that is made is important - from when to get out of bed in the morning to buying a new home: or from visiting the bathroom to visiting family relatives. The impact of these decisions can be wonderful or catastrophic, and everything in between. So here's my business advice:-

1. Use the Business Cube to think through data/information/knowledge needed.
2. Use the Decision Matrix to assess current decision-making in your business.
3. Use the Logical Levels Model to align thinking at the right level for all the Russian Dolls.
4. If you're the Boss, set the example with your decision-making behaviour.
5. If you're part of the Workforce, get used to making more decisions for yourself and others.
6. Every decision deserves the same level of detail and attention: stop making decisions on auto-pilot!

There's a lot more that could and has been written about decision-making, much of it based around organizational design and decision-making structures (such as RAPID). Just cut to the basics - understand why wrong decisions are made in your business, and implement all of the above points.

One book that advances better decision-making is 'Decide & Deliver', written by three employees of Bain & Co., the global management consulting firm. Worth reading!

QUESTIONS - **DECISION-MAKING**

A few quick questions about Section 4.

Q1. Which Cube do you use to better understand your business? _____

Q2. What is the problem of using 'Decision Lite'? _____

Q3. How would you know if a Manager is 'thinking at the wrong level'? _____

Q4. What are the three dimensions of the Decision Cube? _____

Q5. What's the title of the recommended book on decision-making? _____

Q6. Why add an 'Ethical' element to decision-making? _____

SUMMARY This Section covers business decision-making for all Russian Dolls. There's a focus on the behavioural and system improvements that will improve the quality of decision-making at every Level.

1. The first improvement is to use the Business Cube to improve quality of data input into decision-making. Then add an 'ethical' dimension to the traditional 'Eisenhower' Matrix: this expands the depth of assessment, and encourages a broader perspective of possible outcomes: what is called a 'Pre-Mortem'.

5. Recruitment and Selection, Succession Planning.

True Stories: I'm sitting in an open-plan office area of a small recruitment company in England. After talking for 20 minutes about my work experience (after 45 years working, you can talk for 20 minutes!), I say, 'Well, I've done all the talking'......so, by inference, it's your turn. The interviewer leans forward in the chair, and says quietly, 'I must say, I do like your tie'.

Whether you're being interviewed at age 16 or 61, the process has remained essentially the same. So let's upgrade to a global business, with a reputation for effective recruitment practices, using the latest tools and techniques.

It's 10.00am. and the recruiter has booked a call (not Zoom!) for a 60 minute interview. Then there's an email saying that there's a computer system 'glitch', and the interview has been re-scheduled for tomorrow. So it's 10.00am. again, just 24 hours later. By 10.13am., I've realised that there's no call, so I go and make a cup of coffee. Then I hear the telephone ringing: back to the desk, pick the phone, and the first words are, 'Why aren't you picking up your phone?'. I didn't get past that interview. As a postscript, we spoke for 25 minutes on the phone, and some of the time was spent calming the interviewer down. The computer 'glitch' had left him with a substantial backlog of calls to make, and we decided it was best for him to make a cup of coffee and relax. The name of the company: Amazon.co.uk. So if you are, please stop out-sourcing your recruitment, because it's hurting your business.

The first interview was for a job that I would have accepted if offered; the second was by chance, and the third was for this book. And very little has changed in nearly half a century. Except for the technical aspects, the psychometrics, the application of Artificial Intelligence (AI), the countless textbooks on how to improve recruitment effectiveness for your business. And the statistics on successful business recruitment, what The Economist calls *"the single biggest problem in business today"* *unsuccessful hiring. The average hiring mistake costs a company $1.5 million or more a year and countless wasted hours. This becomes even more startling when you consider that the **typical hiring success rate of managers is only 50 percent.***

So this Section will focus on what needs to be done differently: and it starts with the Business Cube. Ask yourself some simple questions: do you need to fill the vacant position? Will filling this position increase sales, reduce costs, or both?: or is it a statutory requirement? Or are you just hiring the best people you can find and then positioning them somewhere in your business? So the first job of the Boss is **think through** the need to recruit: and that means thinking at the 'Who' Level in the Logical Levels Model, the 'Identity'. Again the Implementation Model supports this approach, and it's another reason why it works so well. Using both the Business and Implementation Models, let's take a 'top-down' approach, because it's that 'top-down' approach of cascading behaviour that impacts all the Russian Dolls.

True Story: I've never analysed any business where the recruitment method has changed for any of the management levels, until you reach the Workforce (No.5 Doll). Then there's a shift towards a foreshortened process, sometimes resembling the management recruitment process, but often very different, yet still complying with the legal and statutory requirements for that country.

The argument here is that it's too expensive to engage a recruitment process which is the same (or very similar) for the Workforce. I would strongly disagree with this proposition. The quality of the workforce is the one of the fundamental building blocks of business success - and business improvement. If you have a potential recruit who is demonstrably better than some or all of your current Workforce, then hire them. Whether on an employee or contractor basis is not a consideration.

True Story: Spending a day with an indirect employee working in a manufacturing plant, I recorded the highest level of productive (value-added) working that I've ever seen (96%). Discussing this with his Boss, he admitted that this was a very productive employee, and he worked on his own because it was difficult for him to 'fit' with fellow employees.

The word 'fit' is critical here. One of the generic criteria that the recruiting process uses is 'fit' or compatibility with other team members. And I'm not talking about a policy of Diversity & Inclusion (D & I): I'm talking about the level of 'performance fit'. If you're planning on 'raising the performance bar' in your business, then there's no better place to start than recruitment. Because this Business Improvement is long-term (long-term equates to 3+ years), and the advice is to start now. If the Boss starts with the Senior Managers, improving their performance through a disciplined and demanding approach, and the Workforce are being recruited with firmer criteria, then, in a few years, the competency and performance levels for the Boss, Senior Managers and the Workforce improve. And if there is a policy of 'Internal' Selection, where the Supervisors are chosen from the Workforce, then the performance improvement starts to accelerate. It's then feasible to consider leading and managing the business through the Senior Managers and Supervisors - the Middle Management level becomes the level of technical/innovative expertise, where future value is added to the business through **experimenting and doing** the core activities with different processes and **thinking**. That's where their true value is added.

One of the strengths of Amazon.com is recruitment (I was probably the exception). *'If you want to work for Amazon.....in the tier of managing the business's strategy, don't think that you can be a high tech drop-out entrepreneur - you had better stay at university and complete an MBA. Last year (2016), Amazon hired MBA graduates in the 'high hundreds' from top tier business schools around the world, according to their director of university programs recruitment, Miriam Park'.* ('Top tier recruitment policy for Amazon', March 2017, Penny Brooks). The same level of attention to recruitment for the workforce is missing. *Amazon has added 175,000 temporary positions since March and plans to add more than 133,000 employees to its ranks over the next several months. These positions are in addition to the 876,000 permanent employees that Amazon employed as of July, and could push Amazon's global headcount — including permanent and temporary hires — **up to roughly 1.2 million workers.*** (Business Insider, Áine Cain & Hayley Peterson, September, 2020). With this many people being recruited into the Workforce, it is almost impossible to have a sophisticated recruitment process. Working with a business that has a strong bias towards efficiency and productivity, Forbes ranked Amazon #2 on its newly released World's Best Employers 2020 list. To compile this year's list, Forbes surveyed 160,000 employees from 750 companies in 58 countries around the world and asked them to rate their willingness to recommend their employers to friends and family. Participants also had to rate their satisfaction with their employers' COVID-19 response, economic footprint, talent development, gender equality, social responsibility, and other factors. Forbes used feedback from Amazon employees working both across our logistics network and corporate offices.

A recent New York Times article stated that the founder, Jeff Bezos, believes that 'harmony is often overvalued in the workplace – that it can stifle honest critique and encourage praise for flawed ideas.' The article claimed that Amazon instructs its workforce to 'disagree and commit – to rip into colleagues' ideas, with feedback that can be blunt to the point of painful, before **lining up behind a decision**'. (https://www.muckrock.com/accounts/profile/colinlecher/ April, 2019).

There are a number of points here. Firstly, Amazon is a demanding employer, focused on performance and productivity at every level. That aligns with my Reward Triangle - the need to focus on performance before politics or personalities. Secondly, the need to 'fit' is downplayed - 'harmony is often overvalued in the workplace'. This is very true. With some employers, there's a need to conform to current performance levels as displayed by your Boss and peers: which is why Amazon have a 'Raising the Bar' manager in place during employment or promotion interviews to ensure that the Amazon standards are maintained or strengthened. Thirdly, all Amazon employees are constantly monitored in terms of personal and team performance: which creates a constant turnover of Workforce members.

True story: Decades ago, long before Amazon was born, we operated a very similar policy in a large restaurant in Central London, employing 123 people. There was one slight difference: added to the 'performance' policy was a diversity and inclusion (D & I) measure, which used to be termed positive discrimination. So there was an equal number of all ethnic groups, male and female, that London has to offer. Over a period 18 months, we shifted the restaurant from a loss-making venture to having more operating profit than all the other UK restaurants combined.

'Amazon is a customer-centric company. It would not be wrong to say that the company is obsessed with customer service'. Jeff Bezos continues to live by the phrase; 'I'd rather interview 50 people and not hire anyone than hire the wrong person'. In terms of Business Improvement, this is the correct approach: even one under-performing hiree can severely impact a Business' performance, especially if that hiree is a Senior Manager or the next CEO. This point is emphasised in the book *'Who: the 'A' Method for Hiring',* by *Smart and Street. 'The 'A' Method stresses fundamental elements that anyone can implement - and it has a 90 percent success rate for hiring the right people. We define an 'A' player this way: a candidate who has at least a 90 percent chance of achieving a set of outcomes that only the top 10 percent of possible candidates could achieve. We're saying that you need to initially stack the odds in your favor by hiring people who have at least a 90 percent chance of succeeding in the role you have defined. Not 50 percent, 90 percent. This will take longer in the short run, but it will save you serious time and money down the road. Then in the second part of the definition we raise the bar. Who cares if somebody has a 90 percent chance of achieving a set of outcomes that just about anybody could accomplish? You don't want to be good. You want to be great, and 'A' players have a 90 percent chance of accomplishing what only 10 percent of possible hires could accomplish'.*

True Story: Placing the right people in the right places is easier said than done. If you're serious about growing your business (if you're still reading this book, then you must be!), then learning the skills to hire effectively is critical. After reading this, find out how you can acquire practical skills - which means practicing recruitment without damaging your own business. Or get a professional recruiter to train you. And there are several **true stories** that attest to this - all of them unprintable, unless I want to be sued.

One of the core strengths of Amazon is their recruitment and selection processes at the management level. Whether it's internal or external, **it works**, in the context of a set of beliefs and values that has been described as *'breakneck-paced, and notoriously cost-conscious, as befits a company that has run only a small profit, or a loss, under generally accepted accounting principles for most of its life as a public company'*. Quoting from an article by Dudovskiy, the ambience at Amazon is *'generally, pushy, combative and bruising organizational culture is perceived as outdated. Nowadays, the popular belief is that workplaces need to be nurturing and encouraging, and managers need to be nice and friendly and treat their employees like family in order for a company to succeed.* **The largest internet retailer in the world by revenue proves this belief wrong'**.

Take McKinsey & Co., one of the world's leading business consultancies. Their recruitment and selection process is rigorous, allowing less than 1% of all applicants to eventually join the Company. Again, there's an Application Screening, sometimes using problem-solving tests: the applicant who passes to the next stage is probably among the top 10% of all candidates. There follows a round of Interviews, split between case studies and personal experience. After these, which take some 2 to 3 months, there may be a job offer. **McKinsey & Company was ranked the top consulting firm to work for in North America** according to Vault.com's 2020 Top 50 ranking.

Two companies, both highly successful, in very different business spaces, both using the **'A' Method**. Both are constantly improving their businesses, with Amazon pursuing an aggressive policy of self-improvement. So there are some clear 'best practices' for recruiting and selecting - but what about the mere mortals who are not looking for 'top' jobs? Most of the participants in any Business Improvement fall into this category, and they have to be assessed using the 'A' Method disciplines. As a BI Manager, **never just accept the Team that are chosen** for your Improvement: take time to interview and evaluate each one.

True Story: More problems have been created by colleagues who were recruited and selected for specific Improvement projects, without being assessed by their direct reports beforehand. So the BI Team start work with almost as many operating problems as the Client company. Examples are in retailing, automobile manufacturing, media, petrochemicals: all these were perfectly avoidable, if somebody had just thought through the consequences of their recruitment actions.

Succession Planning

Today's announcement by Amazon that Jeff Bezos will be succeeded by Andy Jassy as the new CEO came after many years of careful and calculated planning [Jeff is currently CEO of Amazon, Andy is the CEO of Amazon Web Services]. So why did it take so long?

Because it's one of the biggest decisions that Jeff Bezos will ever make, allowing him to become Executive Chairman of Amazon's Board. And it's at the Boss and Senior Management levels that most people believe that Succession Planning is only relevant. That's not true. The process is relevant for all the Russian Dolls, at every level: and it starts at the Workforce Level.

True Story: Following the installation of an computerized stock replenishment system, a number of employees were made redundant. A few weeks later came the realization that the new system was flawed, that it consistently underestimated the required manufacturing quantities, and the business was rapidly going out of business. As there was no 'Plan B' in place, then there were no replacements for those people who were made redundant: so they had to be re-hired, at substantial extra cost, having collected their redundancy package. Always have successors lined up for every position, whether it's a part-time cleaner or Chairperson of the Board.

From the Workforce, there will be chosen a few candidates for the Supervisory level - this is internal succession planning, and will always take precedence over the external prospects. This is because it forces your business to develop the best selection process possible, based on 'performance' criteria. At this juncture, at the level that crosses from Supervisory to Middle Management, then 'Personality' and 'Political' considerations become factors in the selection judgement, but 'Performance' will always be the most important element. And every position will have a replacement identified.

True Story: The same discipline applies for BI Teams. On one Business Improvement project, a key member of the Team simply vanished, taking all the Client's work and data with him: there was no back-up, no replacement, so all the work had to be re-done, creating enormous problems.

As the positions in the business become more senior, so the role of Human Resources (HR) starts to emerge. As if by magic, it's assumed that competency in handling the payroll leads to some divine understanding of management and leadership capabilities in individuals. Armed with a selection of psychometric tests, personality assessments and evaluations, the Boss finds certain candidates are quietly promoted at that Middle Manager level, just below the Senior Managers, just out of direct contact. When implementing Business Improvements, the role and influence of HR should be minimal: fine for overseeing DBS checks, (Disclosure and Barring Service, a UK Government Home Office Service), but having limited involvement in recruitment and selection. Best that these skills are learnt by Managers and Supervisors.

True Story: The above advice is based on 35 years of BI experience. The underlying concern of many HR Departments is that a BI generates change, which can create a lack of harmony in a business. Harmony, agreement, consensus are all 'big' issues, and anything that jeopardizes this threatens the natural balance of a business. This is one of the main causes of inertia in any business: Amazon constructively fight against this atrophy. So should your Business Improvement. And beware the HR Department that offers to transfer one of their people into your BI Team to expedite any 'people' issues: they will be reporting on the BI Team performance in detail to their HR Boss.

All this HR information will be inside the Business Cube, ready to be included in the Implementation Model. This means a realistic Succession Plan. Very few businesses have taken the time and made the effort to create this. So get started now!

A few quick questions about Section 5.

Q1. What does 'The Economist' think is the biggest single problem today? _____

Q2. Which US company did Jeff Bezos found? _____

Q3. What does 'Raise the Bar' mean within the Amazon company'? _____

Q4. What is the 'A' Method?_____

Q5. Which other famous American consulting company uses the 'A' Method ? _____

QUESTIONS - **SUCCESSION PLANNING**

Q6. Which Russian Doll level does not use Succession Planning? _____

Q7. Does a BI Team need to Succession Plan? _____

Q8. Why is Succession Planning always important?_____

SUMMARY   This Section covers recruitment and selection at all levels - that means all the Russian Dolls. The reason is simple: **'The most important decisions that businesspeople make are not what decisions, but who decisions'** (Jim Collins, Author of '*Good To Great'*, 2001). It precedes the short section on Succession Planning.

1.   There's a focus on using the best recruitment and hiring techniques, namely the 'A' Method. Although there are dozens of psychometrics that are available, for the purposes of a BI Team and your business, make hiring decisions yourself, and train others to do likewise. This is a cornerstone of building sustainable business improvements.

2.   Succession Planning is a critical activity both for the business and the BI Team. This is a management responsibility that cannot be delegated at any level of Russian Doll. And the closing question: who do you think Jack Ma (CEO) will choose to succeed him at Alibaba? Please forward your answers to me. (nickcbjones59@gmail.com)

6 From <u>Understanding</u> to Implementing

Habit 5: 'Seek first to understand, then to be understood' (Courtesy of Steven Covey[28])

This is the 5th Habit from Steven Covey's book 'The 7 Habits of Highly Successful People', first published in 1989. I've always agreed with this assertion, and wanted to take it further, changing the words slightly.

'Seek first to understand, then to implement': and that's the theme of this Section. The Business Cube does all the 'understanding' of your business, and will highlight which activities need improving, and what impact that could have on all other areas of the business. The Implementation, how the actual Business Improvement is delivered, involves the Russian Dolls and the Logical Levels Model. When the connection between the Cube and the Implementation Model is made, the combination can be viewed as a Business Improvement Model (BIM). Within this context, it's now possible to use a variety of Business Improvement Tools to deliver the financial benefits. And this can be done with an **understanding** of what the impact would be on the rest of the business.

True Story: One Improvement Project in a very large production plant involved the use of some well-known Japanese manufacturing techniques. These were well executed, and showed localized benefits, which were swamped by the overall financial under-performance of this global business. There's a need to see the bigger picture, which can be forgotten or ignored.

So let's take the Business Cube and align it with the Implementation Model:-

Understanding before Implementing

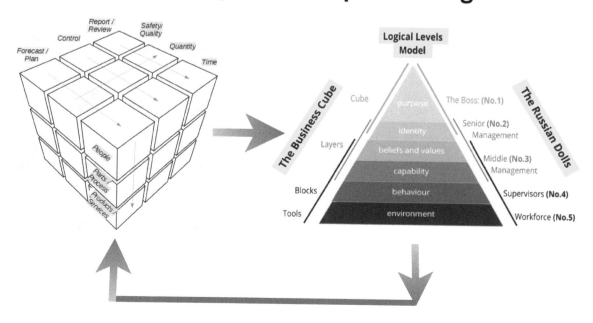

Business Improvement Results

Taking one typical Business Improvement, I'm going to compare the Business Cube approach to the current BI favourite tool, Lean Six Sigma, and I'll start with it's definition.

It's defined as 3.4 defects per million opportunities. Six Sigma...reduces the possibility of variation in production. The objective is to have a firm grasp on the production process. Lean Six Sigma is a term often associated with Six Sigma. Lean methods are used to minimize wastage during production; this includes time and resources spent on processes that do not directly contribute to better output from activities. **Lean Six Sigma is a philosophy** that brings together waste minimization and production optimization. It improves customer satisfaction by removing unnecessary processes and waste, creating better work-flows, faster output, and possibly a competitive advantage. (Courtesy of *Invensis: Global Learning Services, 2021*)

Sitting at the front-end of Lean Six Sigma process is the DMAIC methodology. **D**efine, **M**easure, **A**nalyze, **I**mprove, and **C**ontrol (**DMAIC**) is a data-driven quality strategy used to improve processes. The letters in the acronym represent the five phases that make up the process. It is an integral part of a Six Sigma initiative, but in general can be implemented as a standalone quality improvement procedure or as part of other process improvement initiatives such as **Lean**.

THE 'DMAIC' PROCESS

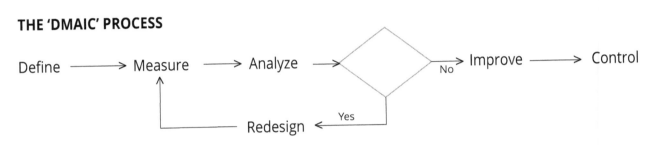

Define the problem, improvement activity, opportunity for improvement, the project goals, and customer (internal and external) requirements: refer to the Project Charter to define the focus, scope, direction, and motivation for the improvement team.
Measure process performance.
Analyze the process to determine root causes of variation and poor performance (defects).
Improve process performance by addressing and eliminating the root causes.
Control the improved process and future process performance.

Lean Six Sigma is a set of business improvement tools, packaged into a comprehensive and professional format. As a BI tool, it is impressive, and has a string of supporters and success stories. Yet there is an 'Achilles heel', a flaw in the process logic, and it lies in the 'Define' step.

Reading the above definition, it seems to fulfil the criteria for starting a Lean Six Sigma business improvement initiative. So what's the problem? Let's ask a few questions:-

1. Have you understood the business issues fully? Have you defined adequately?
2. Does the Project Charter capture all the relevant criteria? Have you missed something?
3. Is Lean Six Sigma the only Business Improvement Tool you need? Is everything you need inside your Toolkit?
4. So what? That infamous question consultants ask to understand exactly what the benefits of the Improvement would be.
5. Are you aligning your 'Definition' to justify a Lean Six Sigma (LSS) intervention? Put simply,

it could be that you have a highly effective BI Tool looking for a business problem to fix or an opportunity to seize.

A recent publication underscores these issues.

'The results of our study point out to significant failure rates for LSS (Lean Six Sigma) projects and alert that projects had higher termination rates in measure and analyze phases (DMAIC – Define, Measure, Analyze, Improve and Control). **Failures occur primarily at the corporate level.** *The main causes of project failures identified were* **lack of commitment by top management, resistance to change, inadequate rewards and recognition mechanisms, inconsistent monitoring and control of the projects, and poor communication.** *Our study shows that there are some minor differences in terms of ranking of these factors between manufacturing and service sectors but there is significant difference in terms of continent and belt level (Master Black Belts, Black Belts, and Green Belts)'.*

Extract from 'A Global study into the reasons for Lean Six Sigma project failures: key findings' by Jiju Antony, Fabiane Letícia Lizarelli and Marcelo Machado Fernandes. Heriot-Watt University, Edinburgh Business School, September 2020.

My contention is that the *higher termination rates in measure and analyze phases* originate in the 'Define' phase: then they manifest themselves in the 'Measure' and 'Analyze' phases. And I would go further and say that the contents of the 'Define' phase are inadequate for their intended purpose. Instead of the 'Define' phase 'zooming out' to capture all the relevant content, it 'starts to 'zoom in', focusing on all the 'Define' Phase elements that are required to kick-start the LSS initiative. By elements, I'm referring to the Process Map, Project Charter, Project Plan, normally consisting of the Resource Plan, Stakeholder Management Plan, Communication Management Plan, Scope Management Plan, Cost/Benefit Plan, and all the Stakeholders' requirements from the LSS. Formidable detail at the 'Front-End' of any LSS.

'Zooming out' is the opposite: take the core of the BI and 'think through' all the elements that will contribute to its outcome. In effect, 'thinking through' is an euphemism for Structured Thinking, and this is best done with a structure. This is where the 'Business Cube' comes into its own. It provides a **structure** and **discipline** to capture all the relevant data/information/knowledge that the BI Leader and Team have to know **before** starting the work: think of this as actually doing a 'pre-mortem'. So there's no need to abandon all the normal elements that occupy the 'Define' phase: just add the Cube in before beginning all this detail.

This approach will highlight any significant obstacles before proceeding, or any hidden benefits and supporters that could become relevant as the BI develops.

True Story: Sitting at my desk in the Client's offices, I received a very friendly email from a colleague. He explained in detail how he'd fulfilled the project charter requirements, and was taking some time-off from the assignment because there was nothing left for him to do. All the remaining work was being transferred to the site that I was based in, hence all the remaining work for me, and he would be 'on the beach' in the afternoon: and he was working in Santa Barbara at the time. Nobody had scoped out the fact that the Client was planning on centralizing their production facilities, so some of their sites became redundant, and some became a lot busier. I was in the busy one. Some of the BI Team members were located in redundant sites, which meant that they too were redundant. If only we had used the Business Cube!

This Story may seem trivial. So let's 'scale-up' the Business Improvement initiatives, and where better to look than the UK Government's list of projects under management. Not all these projects are Business Improvements: in fact, only a fraction of these Improvement Projects are business-focused. This is what Nick Smallwood, the Director of the Infrastructure and Project's Authority (IPA) wrote in his latest Blog. In this article titled *'Setting up for Success: The Importance of Front-End Loading'*, he says *'we must not neglect the importance of **getting the basics right in how we deliver projects.** That is one of the reasons why we recently published the **eight principles for project success**, a quick guide for project delivery professionals on things to get right for any project to succeed. The principle that stands out to me is principle number two; **"plan realistically".** We must i**nvest time in thorough up-front planning to ensure that projects are deliverable and affordable** before commitments are given. No amount of good engineering, management, and construction will provide much resilience if a project was the wrong one to begin with and even good project management will not recover the needed value in a poorly selected project'. '**That is why we need to target the front end of projects.** In this context, **front-end loading refers to the implementation of robust planning, design and preparation for project execution in the early stages of a project's life-cycle to improve the potential for a successful project'.***

Posted by: Nick Smallwood[29] on 9th September 2020 - Infrastructure and Project's Authority (IPA) website, Categories: Construction, Infrastructure, Project Delivery, Project Delivery Profession.

The Business Cube is positioned at the 'Front-End' of the Project Delivery process: it's designed to encourage the Team leader and Members to think through the improvements (or changes) that are planned for the product/service, and understand the consequences of their actions for all Blocks in the Cube. Taking the eight Principles guiding the IPA, they are:-

Principle
	1:	Focus on outcomes
	2:	Plan realistically
	3:	Prioritise people and behaviour
	4:	Tell it like it is
	5:	Control scope
	6:	Manage complexity and risk
	7:	Be an intelligent client
	8:	Learn from experience

All of these Principles are valid: they are helpful as a guidance for those managing Projects. And behind each of these Principles are four key points. No point in listing them, because you can find them on https://www.gov.uk/government/organisations/infrastructure-and-projects-authority.

Comparing these Principles to the Business Cube, particularly with the IPA Project Initiation Routemap, then certain weaknesses appear in the IPA model. Firstly, **lack of structure** - the eight Principles seem to run in sequence, as do the Key Points - but my experience tells me that there has to be a clear and complete approach, with nothing falling between the metaphorical cracks. Secondly, **lack of discipline** - if the Improvement Managers miss facts within 'Principle 2 - Plan realistically', then there's little chance of discovering the 'gap' at an early stage. With the Cube, the 'Forecast/Plan' runs through all 3 Layers (People, Parts & Process, Products & Services), and 9 Blocks. Failure to

Forecast/Plan in any of the 9 Blocks quickly becomes apparent: even missing a small item is flagged up through using **traceability**. Remember that all the Business Improvement parts are within the Cube - there's nothing positioned outside. Same can be said for a Business, or a Project that may not be generating Improvements, just a replacement product or service. Saying that there's a *'need to target the front end of projects'* is correct - actually making that happen is not so easy.

With this type of Business Model, every Project within the IPA portfolio can be understood along three parameters - Resources, Management Systems and Standards. And that gives the ability to benchmark against common dimensions - so Projects that are very diverse by their nature, can be assessed by the same criteria. The typical criteria - for example 'Revenue and Costs - are captured within the Cube: and this allows **transparency** and **traceability** of these measurements through the whole project life-cycle, because the whole project is inside the Cube. So it's very difficult to mix different measures as the Project progresses - such as using Imperial measurements mixed with Metric measurements when building a spacecraft. Or building a sea ferry before you've finished designing it. From my experience, these 'errors' are tangible, they are real, and they do happen, and in hindsight they seem incredible. They may be deliberate or accidental, but current Project management systems are failing to detect the problems in time. With the Cube, enter the project details in the relevant Blocks (such as a Skills Matrix in Block 1, 'People', 'Management Systems' and 'Standards'), then see whether this can be traced through the remaining 8 Blocks (Skills Matrices are just in the 'People' Layer). is it a Key Indicator? Is it on the Project scorecard? Does it just cover the Russian Dolls at the Supervisory and Workforce level? Whatever the personal details inside the Matrix, it can now be seen at the Project macro-level - in the context of the whole Project, not just a stand-alone entity that is occasionally updated. By using a generic template across all IPA Projects, it's feasible to compare across industry groups, or businesses.

True Story: There are several, very human, issues with using the Cube. Firstly, it can expose weaknesses in the logical thinking behind specific Projects or Improvements, which means that options preferred by vested interests can be undermined. Secondly, when problems emerge during the life-cycle, there's a tendency to cover-up the problems, which can then escalate into a major issue. The Cube encourages openness at the **Front End** of projects: so the Risk Analysis becomes a true presentation of business and commercial reality. Then there's the human tendency to tell people what they want to hear, especially the Boss: it's what I call the **'Get Along' Principle**. Right now, there's a **'GAP'** problem with my Local Fire Prevention Officer: he strongly believes that getting along with people is his primary duty. I disagree with him.

Taken in isolation, and on a small scale, the above problem can be managed, but only if you're operating within a working environment that tolerates and accepts this behaviour. The Cube is an intolerant Model: it's a structured and disciplined Model using three dimensions, Resources, Management Systems and Standards. The framework focuses on the **Controllable Drivers**: the levers driving performance within Business Improvements and other types of Projects. So there are many Business Improvement Tools (BITs) that can be used inside the Cube, but switching from one format to another can be quickly detected: put simply, the Standards that are used in the different Layers will be consistent throughout all Layers. Too often you find that Standards can fluctuate, such as in the accounting profession. The same applies to Management Systems that use Key Performance Indicators based on different databases and definitions. The Boss thinks he's comparing 'apples to apples' on his scorecard: sometimes he's not even comparing 'apples to fruit'. And don't think that computerizing or automating systems eliminates or reduces the problem: it just embeds the fundamental flaws more deeply into the BI.

Within this framework, the understanding that is required by the five Russian Doll levels is now more focused: focused on what they need to do at every level in order fro the Bi to be successful and sustainable. Instead of relying on a 'top-down' approach from the Boss, there's now a Cube that encourages accurate data/information/knowledge being fed into the Implementation Model - basically, if it's poor quality, then expect the Implementation to be poor.

So before you implement, there's a need to understand - **understood!**

QUESTIONS - **UNDERSTANDING**

A few quick questions about 'Understanding' in Section 6.

Q1.   What was Steven Covey's 5th Habit? _____

Q2.   What does the 'D' in DMAIC stand for? _____

Q3.   How is Six Sigma defined? _____

Q4.   Which two key elements does the Business Cube provide ? _____

Q5.   What is the 'GAP'? _____

SUMMARY   This is a two-part Section, covering 'Understanding' then 'Implementing'. The clear message is that there is no Implementation before there is a complete Understanding - and that Understanding is data-driven, not an emotional or 'gut' response to instinctive improvements. As I would paraphrase it, 'The numbers set you free'!

1.   The Business Cube strengthens the 'Define' phase in the DMAIC model - and this first phase is one of the main causes of BI problems reflected in the 'Measure' and 'Analyse' phases. Using Lean Six Sigma is a powerful Improvement Tool: just need to ensure that it's leveraged fully through understanding the whole Business opportunity.

2.   Remember that understanding a business requires accurate quantification of the levers that are driving both sales and costs. Having a mastery of the 'numbers' is critical before implementing anything. So make sure you can 'trust the numbers' before introducing the date/information/knowledge into the Implementation Model.

6.1 From Understanding To <u>Implementing</u>

By pure coincidence, I sent an email to a UK Government Department a few days ago and received a prompt reply - non-automated. The respondent clearly hadn't read my email, so the reply was not related to my email contents. And that's the first problem: implementing, or writing a reply, before understanding what you're saying or doing.

If this problem was confined to just emails, then fine: little harm done. But this way of thinking is more deeply ingrained. Most of the actions we take are performed on auto-pilot: unfortunately, Business Improvement initiatives are not one of the activities that can be successfully delivered on auto-pilot.

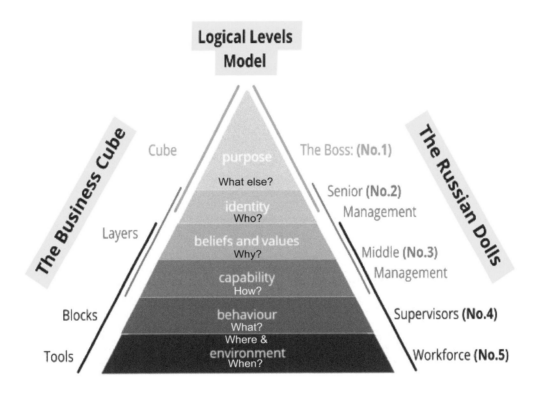

Looking at the above Model, it combines the questions that are linked with each of the Logical Levels. That is the link between the Business Cube and the Implementation Model: the information transferred needs to answer the questions posed within the six Levels.

'What else?' is the key question that the Boss has to consider: so the information has to feed the Key Business Indicators, which have to be a timely and accurate statement of the business's performance and the Business Improvement progress. The two are closely linked: all too often, the BI is seen as a separate entity, and that's one of the biggest mistakes the BI Manager can make. Business events overtake BI benefits. So the BI becomes progressively redundant, without the the BI Team even being aware.

True Story: This top-level Dashboard should be summarized on one side of A4 size paper: behind that daily/weekly summary should be a comprehensive understanding of where every piece of data/information has been derived from, how it's defined, what it means, and what you should do

43

differently if the numbers change significantly. If the numbers change, and the actions remain constant, then why bother reporting it to the Boss. It's critical that the BI gets on the Boss's Dashboard, which means adding to an existing document or creating a new report. On one BI assignment, the Boss needed to drive Improvements continuously, and used the report as a bedrock to keep posing the same question, **'What else**...do we need to do differently?

So the Dashboard data is not just a 'roll-up' from other reports: it needs to prompt thought and action about the BI., and about how it fits within the broader improvement of the business. The 'Amazon' approach to this is very effective, and requires an 'in-depth' understanding of the issues and logic behind the BI. Another approach is to use the '5 Why' technique to deep-dive into understanding the numbers.

'who?' is a critical question. Effective leadership is a key ingredient for successfully implementing any BI. By now, there will be a realization that the quality of questions that are asked, and which interrogative is used, is important. Those questions have to be built on solid data/information/knowledge: this is the bedrock of sound business management and Improvements. Without this, no matter how smart and talented the Boss and Top Team are, they will never get the decisions consistently correct. They might hit a few 'home runs', but that's all.

So the Business Cube has to contain information about the **performance** of the BI Manager and Team Members. Usually this kind of information passes through the prism of the HR Department: I've always preferred to get it direct. So there's a need to listen to what is being said, look at what's being written, and think about aligning the individual within the Improvement Team to deliver optimum results. It's not about working hard, with long hours, it's about working smart.

True Story: Sometimes you have to be patient. There were some serious problems with one business improvement. The savings were evident, but not being acknowledged. So we waited until the right moment, when the 'tipping point' had been reached, and then identified and confirmed those benefits. This is a judgement call for the BI Leader.

Once a week, Andy Jassy[44] calls a meeting to track performance at Amazon Web Services (AWS), the retail giant's cloud computing arm which Jassy has led since the early 2000s. In the meeting the 53-year-old grills each team on its achievements. "He has very high standards," says someone familiar with the event. "You need to know what you're going to present and be ready for him to dive really deep into the details and pick apart what you're saying."... This article in 'The Telegraph' newspaper underlines several reasons for Andy Jassy's recent promotion to be CEO of Amazon, replacing the Founder, Jeff Bezos. What is sometimes overlooked are the operating policies that allow Jeff to pick the best managers, what's been called *Amazon's 'frictionless' ecosystem driving growth. 'Amazon often reviews its organizational structure and pushes out executives when necessary....Either way, the void left by these executives shouldn't be a concern for Amazon, Thomson added, because of its deep bench of talented executives who can fill in those positions immediately'.* There is an Amazon philosophy of 'strength in depth' at every level of the organization: So when the **Who?** question is asked, there are several answers.

Why? is my favourite question: just letting senior and middle managers explain the beliefs and values they hold about the work they're doing, or their current employer, provides a fascinating insight into Business Improvements. And there are two immediate points to be made. Firstly, practice the **art of listening**: you need to listen without interrupting or interjecting, what I refer to as **Active**

Listening, noting all the key points being spoken. Then there's the revelation that the speaker is telling you the facts as understood by them. Their perception of reality is critical to the success or failure of the BI: and they don't lie. One might expect a certain prevarication, or even deception, but no. I'm not a psychologist, but I think it's because nobody has ever asked these types of questions before. So the surprise of the unexpected!

How? sets out the business policies for achieving a successful BI: it explains the criteria and parameters for delivering the BI, and often describes the mechanics of generating the business benefits. So Capability is critical here: do you have the skill-sets, the equipment and technological know-how to actually deliver the BI? The Middle Managers and Supervisors have to ask themselves this question before starting, before creating a BI Plan, or even a Project Plan. This questioning often doesn't happen - and that can create a gap between Top Team expectations and the gritty reality of delivering the BI. So there has developed a myriad of management tools to counteract this problem - from brainstorming to 'thinking outside the box' to contingency planning. And a lot of money has been made by business consultants in delivering and facilitating these training and development programmes.

Which is where using the 'Cube Lite' comes into play (Business Cube Process Flow, 10a). Go back to re-examine the logic behind the BI. Having completed this in-depth study before starting the BI, it's relatively easy to identity problems developing before they become major issues. Depending on the BI life-cycle, this 'Cube-Lite' thinking may be weekly, or every fortnight, or every month. It may last an hour, a shift, a day, whatever it takes to critically think through the latest progress and events. And there's no need to go off-site: in fact, it's better to stay on-site. If it's a multi-site BI, then be at the most important site, where maximum value is are being added.

True Story: For a medium-sized project, it's best to plan any 'Cube Lite' review for a Thursday afternoon, say 2 hours duration, from 2.00pm to 4.30pm., with two 15 minute breaks in between. Involve Middle Managers, Supervisors and key skilled Team Members, to a maximum of 8 people: and work your way logically through all the boxes in the Cube, remembering to start with 'People, Plan/Forecast, Safety/Quality'. I used this approach for one BI project that was nearing completion, undertaken by a different set of consultants, and discovered that the Client was gradually being driven out of business by adopting a work-scheduling software to manage their flow of work.

What? defines the activities of the BI: all of this forms the basis of the BI Plan, the Microsoft Project Plan, or whatever planning software you've inherited or decided to use. This Plan has to be owned by the Supervisors and Workforce: it should **never** be imposed by Middle or Senior Managers. The Managers are responsible for setting up the conditions for a winning BI: for using the Business Cube to logically explore the opportunities and potential pitfalls of the whole Initiative. So one question that the BI Leader should always be asking is, 'Are my people thinking at the right Level?' Are Middle Managers thinking about 'Capability' and aligning their Beliefs and Values, as well as their Supervisors' Beliefs and Values, with the goals of the BI? Once you have the answers to these simple questions, then, as the BI Leader, take the appropriate actions to align all the Russian Dolls with the Levels they should be thinking at.

Where? & When? are exactly as stated. In neuro-linguistic terms, we're at the 'Environment' Level, so these two questions are delivery critical for the BI. Remember that they both flow down from the Levels above, and are the culmination of actions and decisions taken much earlier. For multi-site BIs., then **Where?** is a key question, and for achieving the Project plan, Budget and Timeline, then **When?** is essential. Instead of making a few comments about Supervisors and the Workforce, I'd recommend watching this episode of 'Grand Designs UK' from November 2010 'A 21st Century Answer to the Roman Villa: Revisited from Series 5: Episode 9'), Belfast, Northern Ireland. 24th November 2010. Now the house is an interesting build, but the process and methodology used by the Project Manager / House Owner is textbook example of how to lead, manage and deliver a new build on-time, in-budget and to agreed quality standards. My advice: watch this, learn 'best practice', and replicate behaviours accordingly.

When it comes to watching televised programmes, Channel 4's 'Lotus: a new dawn'[31], brings a different insight. 'If you think about what we have to achieve, it would send you slightly mad' says Matt Windle, newly appointed MD of Lotus Cars based in Norfolk. [He started his career with Lotus in 1998 as a CAD designer. Before re-joining the company to head up the Engineering division in 2017, Matt worked internationally with both high and low-volume manufacturers, including Caterham, Tesla and Volvo]. If only Matt had been using the Business Cube Model: he would have been able to organize his thinking around delivering the last petrol-driven Lotus car together with the first battery-driven Lotus car at the same time. And the Implementation Plan would have reflected a more focused execution of activities / events.

By focused, I mean this. When there's a very tight BI schedule to complete, then every activity step is critical in terms of the Cube dimensions - that's Standards, Management Operating Systems and Resources. So when the Channel 4 camera team are walking behind the Lotus manager as they tour the new car manufacturing plant, they pass two 4ft. x 3ft' white display boards on the left hand side. One board is empty, the other has been meticulously marked with black tape, and is still empty. Having mounted dozens of these type of boards in my working life, I know how long it takes to do this. So why divert people to set-up two boards that are not being used? And this theme is repeated throughout the documentary: which is allowable, if you're not working to a very tight schedule.

Very few viewers would have had these thoughts when watching a very enjoyable programme about car manufacturing in the UK: and that's the opportunity for business improvement in the UK. No matter the industry or business you're improving, are **you** looking and learning what the competitive advantages are for your business.

This is where we can take the Business Cube and Implementation Model and use them to analyse some impending Business Improvements that need to happen for those businesses to survive. Perhaps if I re-phrased that sentence to read…. 'to prosper': or is that a too generous interpretation. Sometimes, there's an article written that captures the essence of my BI argument: an example comes from the Quora website in answer to a business student's question about competition.

Question: **What should a manager do when his business is facing a tough time from competitors?**
Reply by Tom Nault, Managing Partner at Middlerock Partners LLC (2016-present). answered in 2020.

'The business should be doing the same thing it should have been doing all along, and that is to **innovate and produce a product or service that's far better than the competition**. Why wait for competition to be standing over you? Just because the pressure is on, **shouldn't mean you're finally doing something about it.** You should always take competition seriously, even when it seems like no threat at all, **you should have seen this coming and done something about it the moment you went into business.**

I've watched company after company over the last three decades not take competitive threats all that seriously. **I'll ask a CEO about their competitors, and the majority assume they are idiots. Never ever assume you're smarter than your competition.** Even when you're growing at a fast pace, it doesn't mean you're necessarily better, it **could be because the market grew, and not because you're beating your competitor. But, when the market grows, so does competition.**

For many companies facing an ominous competitive threat, doing something about it may in fact be too late. **If you can still survive, then you better get busy coming up with an advantage that will appeal to your customers.** It doesn't matter if you're growing, take competition seriously at all times. **Don't assume that just because your numbers are better that your competitors aren't gaining.** Even when you don't see growth, money could be spent by them on R&D or an acquisition strategy that will leave you stranded.

From the day you're in business, it's your responsibility to build the best company possible and offer something far better than your competitors, and even if they don't seem to be catching up, don't slow down, even for a second. If they are bigger than you, move faster than them. If they are slow to respond, shift when they can't. **Do whatever you have to do to remain better. You otherwise will be either be put out of business or acquired for less than you wished.'**

I would agree with all these points. But so what? They simply remain words spoken or written without a clear alternative as to how to deliver the Business Improvements. And that's where the Cube becomes useful. It provides a structure and process that encourages the business manager to think through their ideas before actually implementing anything. So there's very little expenditure to assess the potential benefits from any BI: you just need to set aside time and thinking power with a lot of focus.

True Story: I spent four days visiting pharmacies and hospitals in South Africa, often in the Townships. The purpose was to consider a new sales and marketing approach for a generic product range, and, after four days, I realised that there wasn't one. So in the de-briefing session with the CEO, I had to tell him that the best business option was to find a commercial arrangement with their main competitor. 'We've already tried that, and they said they'd be taking us over anyway'. And two year's later, the competitor did exactly that. Don't leave it too late to differentiate and improve.

Let's move the Business Cube and Implementation Model forward by reviewing some of the past, present and probably future Case Studies. One past example was BlackBerry Limited, which is now a cybersecurity company specializing in enterprise critical event management solutions, endpoint protection, and securing the Internet of things. A current example include a heating and plumbing business and a software developer, both in the UK: and a future Case Study may include a UK College, which seems an unlikely BI example, so wait to be surprised.

In these four examples, I will show how using the Cube and Implementation Model benefited the BI and Client's business. And I'm delighted to say that never once did my sponsors or employers question the methodology: but some Clients did, so the Case Studies are dedicated to their critical input in developing both the Cube and Implementation Models.

7. Case Study 1: BlackBerry Ltd.

BlackBerry Limited[32] 'provide intelligent security software and services to enterprises and governments around the world', according to their filed Accounts in 2020. And their journey from 1984, when they were founded as 'Research in Motion' (RIM) Limited, has been tumultuous. In a well-documented story, the Company developed the BlackBerry 850, a breakthrough product born in January 1999. In the immediate years that followed, the brand grew in terms of units sold and revenue generated, offering something all its competitors couldn't touch: the ability to email on the go. By 2007, it was the most highly valued Company in Canada.

From that year onwards, the Company began to unwind, to succumb to competitors' products that were demonstrably a better device than the BlackBerry equivalent (Read 'Losing the Signal: The Untold Story Behind the Extraordinary Rise' by Jacquie McNish and Sean Silcoff). This rapid decline has formed the basis of many business Case Studies over the years, and the one by the Harvard Business School is probably the most comprehensive.

Around this time, I had eventually put together a Business Model that would help with my Improvement assignments - often tricky BI projects that required something more than a single Tool. Using the same Business Cube format, I started to pull data and information from the BlackBerry story as it unfolded. Over the weeks, this comprised a lot files, mostly of opinions from business pundits and 'tech' gurus, with some surprising results.

Because the Cube is focused on the essentials for Improvement, it tends to discard data / information that other experts find fascinating at the time. And the first surprise was that BlackBerry were busy implementing exactly the wrong strategy. So let's understand why.

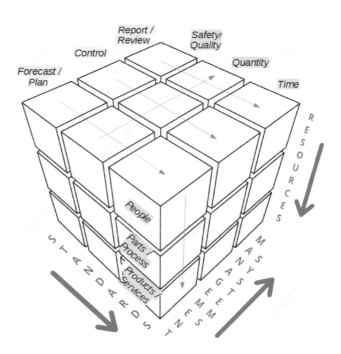

The 'People' Layer form the first 9 Blocks - starting with Forecast/Plan. Ask some basic questions: are there the required skill-sets? Is there a flexible forecast for a rapidly expanding market? Do you always have 'Plan B' for the unexpected business surprise? So the first layer is a real challenge. That's before getting to the third Layer - the BlackBerry product challengers were fundamentally different products. To draw an analogy, today's electric cars look exactly like their petrol and diesel counterparts - except that beneath the skin they are completely different. Same applies to the BlackBerry and Android operating systems - they were fundamentally different.

So the business solution was to create a completely separate business to BlackBerry, quietly identifying key people with the right Android skills to poach from rival companies. Similar to the current strategy employed by Red Bull (the F1 racing team) to poach skilled engineers and mechanics from the Mercedes Team - and both Teams are in exactly the same market segment with very similar products.

Instead, BlackBerry decided to pursue a strategy of product upgrade and improvement that led to *'cyclic adaptation misalignment'* (The Downfall of Blackberry, Ali Moussi, Universteit van Amsterdam). Or constantly failing to deliver a product and service that consistently beats their competitors' products. So why did BlackBerry opt for this incremental product improvement strategy? Because both of the founders came from a technology/engineering background, so there's a 'comfort zone' mindset that underpinned a lot of key business decisions in the BlackBerry business at that time. This tendency to perceive BlackBerry as a 'Technology' business, compared to a customer-driven business, explains much of the BI rationale. So the technology bias came from the Leadership Team (Russian Dolls No. 1 and 2), and was critical to influencing decision-making for many years.

So 'People' and 'Products and Services' are the two key Layers: 'Parts and Process' were never a dominant issue. Now, which BI Tools would you have used to unlock the best strategy for BlackBerry? With hindsight, there's a myriad available, ranging from SWOT (Strengths, Weaknesses, Opportunities and Threats) to PESTEL (Political, Economic, Social, Technological, Environmental and Legal analysis) to Porter's Five Forces. And now there are professional services that help you prepare Case Study answers for leading business universities, like Harvard. To quote from their publicity literature...

In our live classes we often come across business managers who pinpoint one problem in the case and build a case study analysis and solution around that singular point. Business environments are often complex and require holistic solutions. You should try to understand not only the organization but also the industry which the business operates in. Porter Five Forces is a strategic analysis tool that will help you in understanding the relative powers of the key players in the business case study and what sort of pragmatic and actionable case study solution is viable in the light of given facts.

The problem is that these Tools provide part of the business picture: to create a complete overview of the BlackBerry business problems at that time, there's a need to stitch these different Tools together. Easier said than done, because these Tools were never designed to talk with each-other. And this is where the Business Cube comes into play. It's designed to incorporate whichever Tools are best suited to better understand BlackBerry: then help you to understand where the Tools fit in the analysis, and whether there are any gaps in the data/information required to make the right decisions. These gaps are often overlooked because BI managers don't realise what it is that they are missing (or you don't know what you don't know). So the Cube acts as a disciplined approach to understanding and analysing both the data you have, and the data that you're missing and that you definitely need.

True Story: The BI Team had thoughtfully prepared an organization chart of the Client's Top Team and Senior Management, which was useful for our first meeting. After reviewing the information, I said, 'can you please show me who the family members are?'. This was a medium-sized company, founded and owned by a Chinese family, so the 'family members' highlighted the real management team making decisions in the organization. This was critical to delivering a successful BI: none of the BI Team were family members.

Once there's a decision to create a separate business, a separate legal entity, to develop a Smartphone based on Android software and technology, then many of the internal issues that BlackBerry faced would have simply faded away. That would have allowed the Smartphone product development team to focus on the technical aspects of their work, and ring-fence their activities from an increasingly volatile management situation. Consider this in the context of the Cube: take the 'People' Layer and then work through the 'Parts and Process' Layer - the Supply Chain, Vendor Base etc., until you reach the 'Products and Services'. The Smartphone is a new product with associated services: then think 'Safety/Quality', 'Quantity' and 'Time'. By completing this Cube approach before attempting a BI Plan (often called a Project Plan), then the chances of producing a relevant and accurate Plan are greatly enhanced. Why?

Because Plans are generated by managers who are under pressure, often personally, and always from a BI benefits perspective. Whether it's a Waterfall or Scrum methodology at work, they both have their inherent weaknesses, because at their heart, the BI Team will be working to the BI Plan, making adjustments to that Plan when they are obliged to. It's this Plan that Individuals and Team are held accountable to deliver: so the more accurate and realistic the planning up-front, the greater the probability of hitting the agree BI Budget, in the agreed timeframe, with the agreed benefits in terms of product and service. This BI Planning is key: and if only I had a crisp $20 bill (or £20 note) for every time a critical element of the Plan has been overlooked at the outset. Even a seemingly trivial item (or line on a Project Plan) can become decisive to achieving BI success. 'The devil is in the detail', a quote from one of my former No.1 Dolls, and never a truer word spoken. The Cube forces the BI Manager to think through the structure and details required for effective Planning.

So I'm kicking off the Case Studies with a decades earlier example that has had countless Business Cases following in its wake. And not one of them ever recommended setting up a separate business to counter the competitors' Android - based Smartphones.

Looking at events over 20 years ago, there's a tendency to fit events into a particular business model - so business case studies will often be geared towards specific 'learning points', whether it's sales and marketing, finance or something more obscure. So let's take a current case study, an ongoing look at one of the 243 Higher Education Colleges in the UK.

If you think that a College is not a business, then why do they have EDITDA (Earnings before Tax, Depreciation and Amortization) as one off their key performance indicators? Somebody in the British Government believes that this business measure is valid, so it becomes relevant, and we are actually looking at a College that is a business, and a business that is shows itself as a College. Let's see how this works with the Business Cube.

Case Study 2: College, UK

So can the Business Cube be of any use? Without too much effort it's possible to modify the Cube format to focus on the **key business Resources.** So identify 'Students with People', then amend 'Parts and Processes' to 'Process Delivery and Products', and lastly change the 'Products and Services'

The Business Cube

The College Cube[33]

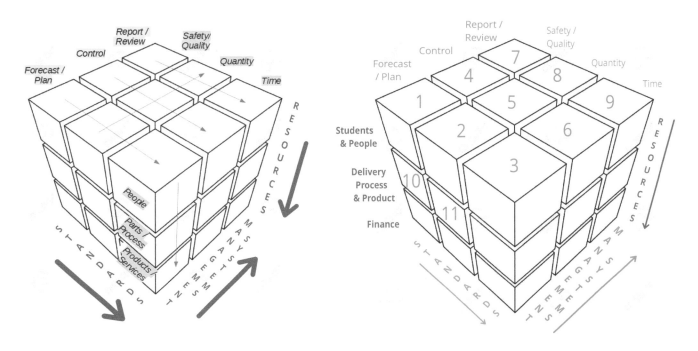

to 'Finance'. That covers the entire scope of the College, and the 'College Cube' works in the same way as the 'Business Cube', exactly the same way.

In this instance, the objective is to broaden the thinking of the Senior Leadership Team by using the Cube to think through structurally the behavioural improvements required to improve **Standards.** So instead of supporting piecemeal improvements, there's a more coordinated approach and delivery: which means understanding how all the 'educational' products fit together in a complete package that can be delivered above OFSTED[34] Standards.

As you can see from the College Cube, both the Standards and Management Systems remain the same as the Business Cube. And the same discipline in thinking can deliver higher standards without 'blood, sweat and tears'.

True Story: Never throw money at a business problem: think first, then act. I spent four days visiting pharmacies and hospitals in South Africa, often in the Townships. The purpose was to consider a new sales and marketing approach for a generic product range, and, after four days, I realised that there wasn't one. So in the de-briefing session with the CEO, I had to tell him that the best business option was to find a commercial arrangement with their main competitor. 'We've already tried that, and they said they'd be taking us over anyway'. And two year's later, the competitor did exactly that. Don't leave it too late to differentiate and improve.

Understanding How We Can Deliver Improved 'Standards' With a College Cube[34]

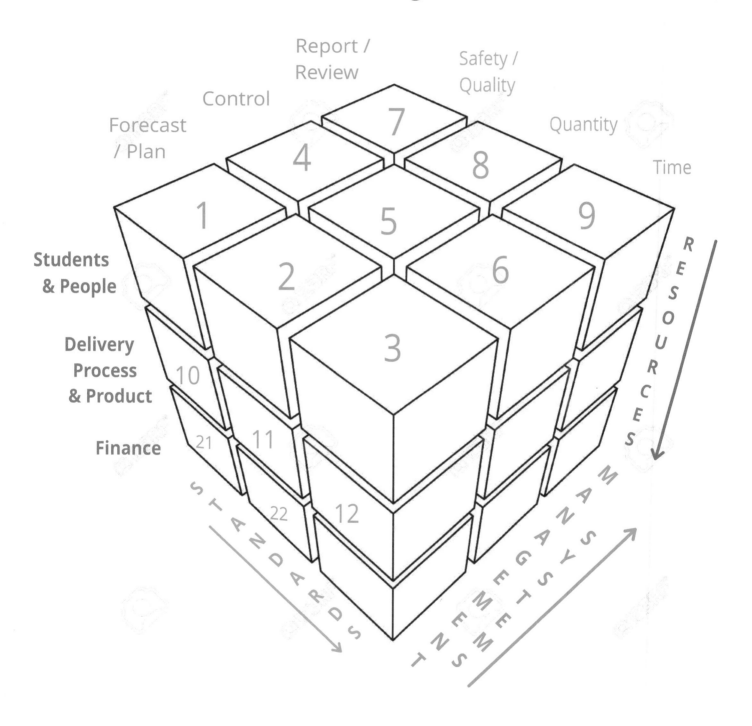

Structured Approach To Improving 'Standards'

Students / People -
1. Students/People, Forecast/Plan, Safety/Quality
2. Forecast/Plan, Quantity
3. Forecast/Plan, Time
4. Control, Safety/Quality
5. Control, Quantity
6. Control, Time
7. Report/Review, Safety/Quality
8. Report/Review, Quantity
9. Report/Review, Time

Delivery Process & Product -
10. Delivery Process, Forecast/Plan, Safety/Quality
11. Forecast/Plan, Quantity
12. Forecast/Plan, Time
13. Control, Safety/Quality
14. Control, Quantity
15. Control, Time
16. Report/Review, Safety/Quality
17. Report/Review, Quantity
18. Report/Review, Time

Finance -
19. Finance, Forecast/Plan, Safety/Quality
20. Forecast/Plan, Quantity
21. Forecast/Plan, Time
22. Control, Safety/Quality
23. Control, Quantity
24. Control, Time
25. Report/Review, Safety/Quality
26. Report/Review, Quantity
27. Report/Review, Time

KEY OPPORTUNITIES FOR 'STANDARDS' IMPROVEMENT

Students / People -

Opportunities	Actions	Who	When	Status		
				Past	Present	Plan
1. Skills Builder						
2.						

Delivery Process / Products -

Here are some examples of possible opportunities to improve 'Standards' in a College.

Opportunities	Actions	Who	When	Status		
				Past	Present	Plan
1. IT Strategy / Cybersecurity						
2. QIP (Quality Improvement Programme)						

Finance -

Opportunities	Actions	Who	When	Status		
				Past	Present	Plan
1. Current Deficit						
2.						

Case Study 3: Heating & Plumbing, UK

This is an example of a small, privately owned business based in the East Midlands, operating in a traditional industry with strong competition. Like many Clients, there was a driving need to address some ongoing business issues: once that's been achieved, then there are questions about growing the business in the region.

Without delving into commercial details, let's say that the issue lies in the 'Parts & Process' Layer, specifically with 'Controlling' activities: so it's centring on **Box 14 ('Parts & Process', 'Quantity' and 'Control')**. Which means the current Process ('way of working') is taking too long to complete for the number of Service / Installation planned visits. And this extra cost of is actually being borne by the business, and is not being built into the financial plan, so planned margins are well in excess of actual margins. At the end of the financial month, the actual profit margin is less than the plan.

So the Cube rules state that you **start with Box 1** when understanding the business: because right at the outset, you never make assumptions about the root causes of problems. And **Box 1 is 'People', 'Safety and Quality', 'Forecasting and Planning'.** So some simple questions to pose:-

1. How many people are working in Operations? - Actual Nos. and Full Time Equivalents.
2. How many are qualified, and to what level? Are they all currently valid?
3. How many hours are being worked by the Operations Team?
4. Is there a forecast for the required hours to be worked against the predicted demand level.

And there are many more questions that follow this Cube approach. As you work your way through the Boxes, a clearer picture emerges of what the fundamental issues are in the business - and remember to work through to Box 27, ('Products & Services', ' Report & Review', 'Time'). That overview highlights where detailed studies and management action needs to be focused. Many times I've seen premature conclusions drawn and actions taken before a reasoned and logical understanding of the Client's business has taken place. And for those veterans of consulting who would argue that the Analysis phase of the Consulting process will do all of this for you, here a few reasons why not.

1. **The Client's going out of business** - they'll be bankrupt if we don't do something now. *Response - If they're going bankrupt, consultants will be the last to be paid, if at all. So why are you working with them? And if you do decide to go ahead, then do a proper job and understand the whole business. From my experience, some business analyses are just plain dangerous - they mislead more than inform.*

2. **The Client's business is too complicated** - *I've never met any business that was too complicated to understand: and this argument is closely followed by 'our business is unique'. No business is unique, except those at the technical 'cutting edge' of their industry or specialism, and they are still subject to commercial forces.*

3. **The Analysis focuses on the Client's perception of their problems** - *So you think Senior Management are the best source for understanding the business's issues? Nowadays, social media can provide insights into a failing business, or listening to their customers, or vendors, or any independent source of commercial knowledge.*

4. **Understand who owns the Client's business** - *Complete Analyses have been completed over a 2 week period, and we still don't know who really owned the business - and by 'own', I mean who is*

legally responsible in which country.

There are many more reasons why an Analysis can mislead rather than inform and guide, and for most consultants an Analysis is simply part of the Sales Process with the Client. So beware Analyses, and rely more on a structured approach using the Cube.

As the weeks progressed, the root causes of the problems were resolved, starting with accurate data collection for costings of products and services. So one of the basic flaws was that planned margin calculations were way too optimistic when compared to the actual costings: there was a need to control costs more tightly and target the highest margin geographical areas and customers. Put simply, the greater the distance travelled from base to customer, the greater the time spent not earning revenue, and increasing costs through extra diesel consumed by the vehicle.

And many business people would say that this conclusion was self-evident, and there's really no need for a Cube approach. Yet the Cube is not just for one major event, for example, identifying costing issues. Another benefit is to prevent or forewarn business people **before** their business gets into commercial difficulties. This 'alarm bell' mechanism is similar to the Amazon.com Inc. approach using SWOT analysis, PESTEL, Porter's Five Forces. ('*Amazon Organizational Culture: harsh, but effectively contributing to the bottom line*', Business Research Methodology, John Dudovskiy, March 2020). The key difference is that these analysis tools can be incorporated inside the Cube - they are mutually supportive and can help you in a more in-depth understanding. But never lose sight of the 'big' picture - and that's where effective leadership becomes a decisive factor in delivering effective Business Improvements.

And our 'Heating & Plumbing' business has effective leadership: coupled with an effective Management Operating System, highlighted as a weakness by a Cube analysis and then some Cube Lite reviews, then there are two fundamental elements of a successful business in place. Improvement becomes so much easier when your business is in a strong and financially healthy position to start with. Remember, **Cube Overview + Effective Systems + Effective Leadership** leads to successful Business Improvements.

Case Study 4: Software Development, UK

Completely different industry and enterprise. This is a one person business, with optional contractors available when required, that specializes in web design, web development and App. design and development. Again, there was a 'trigger' some years ago that prompted the owner to critically examine what the business was doing and how they were doing it. Given that they are very technically competent in their field, then the issues were more commercially driven. And the Cube approach was used to understand the overall business performance initially, then delving into a more progressively detailed understanding.

Use the Cube Model to take the Client through the process step-by-step, or box-by-box. Ensure their understanding of this structured process: then use the Implementation Model to engage the Business Improvements. In this case, we used the Logical Levels Model (LLM) to clarify the Client's thinking at the 5 different Levels, starting with 'Environment'. From this came the realization that the Client loved the technical aspects of their work, the mechanics of software writing, and not so much the development of their business. And that was one of the root causes of the issues: more time and resources had to be spent **on the business, not in the business.** Once the Client acknowledges that reality, then behaviour changes, and similar business problems do not recur.

Future Case Study 5: Ecommerce

There's an excellent book on business conducted through e-commerce *(The Economics of E-Commerce: A Strategic Guide to Understanding and Designing the Online Marketplace by Nir Vulkan, Princeton University Press, 2020). '...e-commerce will have major and lasting effects on economic activity. But the rise and fall in the valuations of the first wave of e-commerce companies show that vague promises of distant profits are insufficient. Only business models based on sound economic propositions will survive. It demonstrates how these tools can be used to assess a variety of existing applications.....This text teaches how to analyze the added value of such applications, considering consumer behaviour, pricing strategies, incentives, and other critical factors. It discusses added value in several e-commerce arenas: online shopping, business-to-business e-commerce, application design, online negotiation (one-to-one trading), online auctions (one-to-many trading), and many-to-many electronic exchanges. Combining insights from several years of microeconomic research as well as from game theory and computer science, it stresses the importance of economic engineering in application design as well as the need for* **business models to take into account the "total game."**

When referring to the 'total game', interpret as the whole business: the Business Cube and Implementation Model work just as well with an Ecommerce background as with the more familiar 'Heating & Plumbing' type of business. Looking at *'How To Start an Ecommerce Business From Scratch' July 16, 2021 / By Darren DeMatas*, here's a generic step-by-step approach:-

1. Research Ecommerce Business Models
2. Start Ecommerce Niche Research
3. Validate Target Market and Product Ideas
4. Register Your Ecommerce Business & Brand Name
5. Finalize Your Ecommerce Business Plan
6. Create Your Online Store
7. Attract Customers To Your Ecommerce Website

Clearly the 2nd and 3rd Actions are very important and, in my opinion, are more important than the 1st Action. Unfortunately, I've never worked with a true Ecommerce Client, but my experience with Misys plc., one of the world's largest independent applications software products groups and the UK's biggest, would lead me to believe that the Cube would fit perfectly into any BI assessment, and the Implementation Model would work in exactly the same effective way when delivering the BI.

Any Ecommerce business that is considering a Business Improvement, and NBJ Business Solutions Ltd. would be delighted to provide insight and support.

Case Studies Summary

There are four live Case Studies, from the large and historical (BlackBerry Ltd.) to the small, single owner (Software Development, UK). Whatever the size and nature of your Business Improvement, the Cube is flexible enough to accommodate very different BIs.

And everything about your BI is inside the Cube - there's no need to think outside the box. And your thinking is prioritised by the People Layer being first - so you actually put People first in your thinking.

And you can have whatever Tools you prefer inside the Cube - there are no exclusions: you just need to think about the Tools you decide to use. All of the Case Studies discussed here had a beneficial impact on the Client's business (except for BlackBerry Ltd.!) - those business owners now see their businesses from a broader perspective, and before the business issues really start to bite.

And on the downside - you are required to think about the BI in a structured and logical way from the outset, and at frequent intervals during the Implementation. And the 'thinking' part is the primary difficulty. Because many business people have successfully established their small or large enterprises, there's a feeling that there's no need to re-think anything: so their BI is simply more of the same 'winning' formula they've been using for years. One word to describe this: flawed! Time after time, BIs have failure built-in to their DNA, from the start, because one factor was overlooked, or maybe more than one. Or the BI was poorly positioned within the business, or had unintended consequences, or was simply **'built-to-fail'.**

The cost of rectifying these mistakes can be colossal for many businesses - some have to re-structure, some go bankrupt, and some are taken over by competitors or VCs. So before you rush into your next bright idea, think it through - use the Cube!

And the Implementation Model. There are a myriad of ways that business owners and managers use to install Improvements. But my recommended approach uses the data coming the Business Cube to maximum advantage. Once the data is confirmed by observations / documentation, then there's a bedrock of facts that form the basis of your BI. Using the 'Russian Dolls' to implement effectively at every level in the organization means involving all participants: there are no forgotten groups, no abstentions, no managers who are never present when required, And the use of NLP does discipline behaviour: it encourages listening before speaking, thinking before doing, and tends to slow-down the headlong rush to **Action Now**.

Because the pressure from the Boss can be overwhelming. The business need to make improvements can be critical, so the BI Leader has to focus on essential data, from which they can make informed decisions.

And the upside - In a word, **winning!** Because you have to get ready for your next BI in order to stay competitive.

Notes:

Page No.:

2. Leadership[1] - Defined as 'the art of motivating a group of people to act toward achieving a common goal'. https://www.thebalancesmb.com

2. Leadership Books[2] - based on an article from https://serveleadnow.com, Cairnway, January 2018, by Joe Iarocci.

4. Resources[3] - https://www.collinsdictionary.com - the resources of an organization or person are the materials, money, and other things that they have and can use in order to function properly.

4. Standards[4] - A standard is a level of quality or achievement (for *Safety/Quality, Quantity and Time*)

4. Management Systems[5] - https://www.yourdictionary.com/management-system - The leadership and control within an organization.

5. Decision-making[6] - Enable a manager to consider alternatives and use judgement to choose an appropriate and timely course of action.

5. Recruitment and Selection[7] - Recruitment is the process of finding people to work for a company. Selection refers to the methods used to choose the best or most suitable candidate for the vacancy.

5. Succession planning[8] - Succession planning is the process of identifying and developing potential future leaders and senior managers, as well as individuals, to fill business-critical roles.

6. 'Failure is not an option'[9] - is the tag line of the 1995 film Apollo 13. It is spoken in the film by Ed Harris, who portrayed Gene Kranz, and said,"We've never lost an American in space; we're sure as hell not going to lose one on my watch. Failure is not an option."

6. Organization[10] - is an entity – such as a company – comprising one or more people and having a particular purpose.

6. Span-of-Control[11] - is the manageable number of subordinates of a superior: the bigger the number of the subordinates a manager controls, the broader is her/his span of control.

6. Skill's Matrix[12] - is a visual tool that helps you to clearly see the skills and competencies of individuals within an organisation.

7. Authority, Responsibility, Accountability[13] (ARA) - https://www.pm-primer.com/authority-responsibility-and-accountability

7. Projex[14] - Projex.com - The Projex Academy provides a simple guide to ARA.

7. Logical Levels Model[15] - www.logicallevels.co.uk/pages/logical-levels-model - outlines the use of the Tool in the UK.

7. Parrots[16] - Unofficially, a group of managers/leaders who oppose the BI Manager and Team.

9. Management Mirror[17] - Courtesy of Caruso Management - 'The Management Mirror: Employees Reflect Management' - Joe Caruso, 3rd February 2016. Recommended reading.

9. Law of Imitation[18] - Courtesy of 'The Laws of Imitation', Leadership by Imitation, June 2013, Comments Off on Leadership by Imitation.

9. Ethical[19] and Legal[19] - Ethics are "a system of principals and customs that affect how people lead their lives". They are different to legislation or laws that legally dictate what is right and wrong. Ethics represent society's opinions about what is right and what is wrong.

9. Management By Exception[20] - (MBE) - is a business management strategy which states that managers and supervisors should examine, investigate and develop solutions for only those issues where there is a deviation from set standards, norms, business practices or any other financial goals like profits deviation, quality issues, infrastructure issues.

12. Thinking systemically[21] - thinking that is related to a system, especially when affecting the entirety of a thing.

13. Thinking systematically[22] - thinking in a focused, consistent, and methodical way.

19. Pyramid Training[23] - inspired by The Minto Pyramid Principle: the Basic Pyramid Concept – why the pyramid structure, its rules, and how the ideas within that structure relate vertically and horizontally, and how to build a Pyramid – how to identify the reader's question, and then use the pyramid rules to discover and organize the points needed to answer that question.

21. Grenfell Tower[24] - now the subject of a Public Inquiry. (https://www.grenfelltowerinquiry.org.uk)

22. The Reward Triangle[25] - Devised to get the BI Team focused on Performance, and away from Politics and Personality.

26. The Eisenhower Matrix[26] - sometimes referred to as Urgent-Important Matrix, helps you decide on and prioritize tasks by urgency and importance, sorting out less urgent and important tasks which you should either delegate or not do at all.

27. The Decision Cube[27] - a three-dimensional approach to making decisions, emphasising the ethical aspect.

37. Steven Covey[28] - he focused on the transforming power of principles rooted in unchanging natural laws that govern human and organisational effectiveness; adapting every aspect of one's life to accord with these principles; effective leadership; and empowerment.

40. Nick Smallwood[29] - is the Chief Executive Officer of the Infrastructure and Projects Authority and Head of the UK Government's Project Delivery Function: former Vice President for Projects Engineering and Chief Projects Engineer at Shell. 40 years experience of managing complex project portfolios and having developed Shell's Global Project Academy. At Shell, he was accountable for managing how projects were delivered and a variety of significant improvement programmes.

44. Andy Jassy[30] - is the president and CEO of Amazon since July 5, 2021. Jassy led Amazon Web Services since its inception in 2003. He replaced Jeff Bezos as president and CEO of Amazon on July 5, 2021, and Bezos became executive chairman.

46. Lotus Cars[31] - available from this website: https://www.channel4.com/programmes/lotus-a-new-dawn/on-demand/73000-001.

48. BlackBerry Ltd.[32] - is a Canadian multinational company specialising in enterprise software and the Internet of things. Originally known as Research In Motion, it developed the BlackBerry brand of interactive pagers, smartphones, and tablets.

51. College Cube[33] - is a derivative of the Business Cube, with an emphais on delivering Improvements for Colleges, not businesses.

51. OFSTED[34] - is the Office for Standards in Education, Children's Services and Skills: they inspect services providing education and skills for learners of all ages.

Key Term's Index:

Bibliography (Alphabetical by Surname)
Published Sources and Recommended Reading

Allcott, Graham, *How to be a Productivity Ninja,* 2014.

Allen, David, *Getting Things Done*, March 2017.

Beddoes-Jones, Fiona, *Thinking Styles: Relationship Strategies that Work!,* 1999.

Beddoes-Jones, Fiona, *Divided by Gender, United by Chocolate: Differences in the Boardroom,* 2017.

Bergin, Tom, *Spill and Spin, The Inside Story of BP,* 2012.

Bevan, Judi, *The Rise and Fall of Marks and Spencer,* 2002.

Blenko Marcia, Michael Mankins, Paul Rogers, *Decide & Deliver,* Bain & Co., 2010.

Clark, Duncan, *The House that Jack Ma Built,* 2016.

Cole, Nussbaumer and Knaflic, *Storytelling with data,* 2015.

Collins, Jim, *Good to Great,* 2001.

Collinson, Simon and Jay, Melvin, *From Complexity to Simplicity,* 2012.

Cruver, Brian, *Enron: Anatomy of Greed,* 2002.

Danoesastro, Martin, *'What are you willing to give up to change the way we work?'* TEDx, Jan 2019.

Dobelli, Rolf, *The Art of Thinking Clearly,* 2013.

Frierstein, Mitch, *Planet Ponzi,* 2012.

Fuda, Peter, *Leadership Transformed: How Ordinary Managers Become Extraordinary Leaders,* 2013.

Garratt, Bob, *The Fish Rots from the Head,* 1996.

Geneen Harold, Alvin Moscow, *Managing,* 1984.

Gladwell, Malcom & Decker,John, *The Tipping Point, How Little Things Can Make a Big Difference,* 2000.

Goldratt, Eliyahu, *Theory of Constraints,* January 1999.

Goldratt, Eliyahu, *The Goal,* 1984.

Goleman, Daniel, *Emotional Intelligence Why it Can Matter More Than IQ,* Sept 1996.

Ghoshal, Sumantra & Bartlett, Christopher, *The Individualized Corporation,* 1988.

Hirano, Hiroyuki, *5 Pillars of the Visual Workplace,* 1995.

Honey, Peter, *50 Cautionary Tales for Managers,* 2006.

Horowitz, Ben, *The Hard thing about Hard Things,* 2014.

James, Oliver, *Office Politics,* 2013.

Jensen, Bill, *The New Competitive Advantage,* 2000.

Krogerus, Mikael & Tschappler, Roman, *The Decision Book,* 2011.

Laloux, Frederic, *Reinventing Organizations,* 2014.

Lewis, Gareth, *The Mentoring Manager,* 1996.

Lewis, Michael, *Liar's Poker,* 1989.

Mant, Alistair, *Leaders we Deserve,* 1983.

Marcouse, Ian & Lines, David, *Business Case Studies 2nd Ed.,* 1994.

Marquet, L.David, and Stephen Covey, *Turn the Ship Around!: A True Story of Turning Followers into Leaders,* September 2013.

Martyr, Tony, *Why Projects Fail: Nine Laws for Success,* 2018.

Mauboussin, Michael, *Think Twice,* 2013.

McLean Bethany and Peter Elkind, *The Smartest Guys in the Room,* 2003.

McNish, Jacquie and Silcoff, Sean, *Losing the Signal,* 2015.

Mintzberg, Henry, *Structure in Fives,* June 1992.

Norton Bob & Cathy Smith, *Understanding Management Gurus,* 1998.

Oliver, Anton, *The Revenue Vault*, 2019.

O'Shea James and Charles Madigan, *Dangerous Company*, 1999.

Osono Emi, Norohiko Shimizu, Hirotaka Takeuchi, *Extreme Toyota*, 2008.

Papke, Edgar, *True Alignment*, Amacom, 2014.

Peters, Steve, *The Chimp Paradox,* 2012.

Pink, Daniel, *When*, January 2018.

Pinker, Steven, *The Stuff of Thought*, 2007.

Radcliffe, Steve, *Leadership: plain and simple*, 2010.

Salaman, Graeme, *Decision Making for Business*, 2002.

Schonberger, Richard, *Building a Chain of Customers,* 1990.

Sinek, Simon, *Start with Why: How Great Leaders Inspire Everyone To Take Action*, 2011.

Singer, Mark, *Funny Money*, 1985.

Smart, Geoff & Street, Randy, *Who - the 'A' method for hiring'*, September 2008.

Smith, Jay, *How Jeff Bezos Built an E-Commerce Empire: The Unwritten Story of Amazon.com*, April 2018.

Sorkin, Andrew Ross, *Too Big to Fail,* 2009.

Stone, Brad, *The Everything Store: Jeff Bezos and the Age of Amazon*, 2014.

Taleb, Nassim Nicholas, *The Black Swan*, 2007.

Thomas, C William, *The Rise and Fall of Enron*, March/April 2002.

University of Sheffield, HR Dep't., *On Recruitment and Selection*, 2018.

Vardy, Adam, *Project Management for Beginners*, 2012.

Articles (Alphabetical by Surname)

Anon, *Self-Directed Work Teams*, MBASkool.com, 2018.

Arrington, Michael, *There is a difference between evil and just being absurdly profitable*, Oct. 2009.

Bassi, Laurie: McMurrer, Daniel, *How's your Return on People,* HBR, March 2004.

Beddoes-Jones, Fiona and Miller, ,Julia, *The Psychology of Teams*, April 2004.

Beyer, Philip, *Why Lean Fails 98% of the Time? The Answer*, System 100, April 2017.

Broni-Mensah, Louise, *'Excellence isn't an act, it's a habit'*, December 2018.

Burgess, Kate, *Collapse of Carillion*, January 2018.

DeMatas, Darren, *'How to Start an Ecommerce Business from scratch'*, July 2021.

Dougal, *CEO Secrets: Recruit people 'better than you'*, BBC, August 2015.

Dudovskiy, John, *Amazon Organizational Culture: harsh, but effectively contributing to the bottom line'*, March 22, 2020

Duhigg, Charles, *Want to be more productive? Think deeper'*, Opinion, Director, May 2016.

Fitzherbert, Teresa, *What Tech insiders really think of Andy Jassy, the soon-to-be CEO of Amazon*, 2021.

Fuda, Peter, *TheDanger of 'Why'?*, June 2021.

Gallup, *The cost of bad project management*.

Gartner, *Survey shows why projects fail*.

Gifford, Jonny, *Performance management: an introduction*, CIPD, September 2018.

Gifford, Jonny, *Could do better? What works in performance management*, CIPD, December 2016.

Gosport Independent Panel, *Gosport War Memorial Hospital*, June 2018.

Harvard Business Review, *Why your IT project may be riskier than you think*.

H of C, Briefing Paper, *The Collapse of Carillion, No. 8206,* March 2018.

H of C, Transport Committee, *Rail Timetable Changes, HC 1163,* June 2018.

Hyacinth, Brigette, *Micromanagement make BEST PEOPLE Quit!,* July 2018.

Iarocci, Joe, Cairnway, *Leadership Books,* January 2018.

IBM / CIO Leadership Office, *Update for TSB Board,* April 2018.

Jacobs, Katie, *Is Psychometric testing still fit for purpose?,* February 2018.

Kim, Eugene, *Top Amazon Exec.,* CNBC Tech, December 2020.

Marquet, L.David, *Turn the Ship Around,* 2012.

Martin, Gary, *Pot Stirrers and Blame Gamers,* May 2018.

McGraw, Karen, *Improving Project Success Rates with Better Leadership,* PM Times, November 2018.

Mindtools, *7 Ways to Use Office Politics Positively,* 2016.

Mintzberg, Henry & Gratton, Lynda, *Top Thinkers,* 2018.

Monaghan, Angela, *Timeline of trouble: how TSB IT meltdown unfolded,* June 2018.

Montag, Ali, *This is Jeff Bezos' 3-question test for new Amazon employees,* August 2018.

Myers Briggs, *Personality Types,* 1948.

Nelson, Robert, *The Leaders Use of Informal Rewards and Reward Systems in Obtaining Organizational Goals,* November 1993.

Oakervee, Douglas, *Oakervee Review,* 2019

Parikh, Tej, *Lifting the Long Tail: The Productivity challenge through the eyes of small business leaders'* Institute of Directors, IoD, (October 2018).

Parkinson, Mark, CIPD, *A Head for Hiring,* 2015.

Persona People Management Ltd., *The Five Key Factors,* 2018.

PMI: Pulse of the profession 2018', Project Management Institute

Porter, Sarah, *Apple,* 2018.

Renoir Ltd., *9 Rules of project management,* 2018.

Reynolds, Paul, *A scheme to increase profitability in entrepreneurial SMEs.,* 2018.

Shaw, Dougal, *CEO Secrets: Recruit people 'better than you',* BBC, August 2015.

Silverman, Lori: Propst, Annabeth, *Ensuring Success: A Model For Self-Managed Teams,* Partners for Progress and Fuller & Propst Associates, 1996.

Strom, John, *Maximizing Your ROPI - Return on Your People Investment,* January 2017.

Swartout, Donna, *Self-Directed Teams: Definition, Advantages & Disadvantages,* Study.com, 2018.

Templer, Klaus, *Personality and Individual Differences,* April 2018.

Terry, George, *Principles of Management,* with Stephen G. Franklin, 1994.

Tesco, *Strategic Report,* 2018.

Vulkan, Nir, *The Economics of E-Commerce: A Strategic Guide to Understanding and Designing the Online Marketplace,* Princeton University Press, 2020.

Ward, Susan, *What is Leadership?,* The Balance Small Business, September 2020.

Wellingtone, *The State of Project Management: Annual survey,* 2018

Postscript

Two postscripts: one on a professional level, and the other personal. Here goes.

On a professional level, The Russian Dolls have fascinated me for years: as an allegory for the hierarchical structure that seems to obsess management teams and businesses, they are peerless. Without the clutter of organization charts, organograms, leadership charts, and even the family tree, it's possible to understand at-a-glance which Level should be asking which questions to whom and when. Asking the right questions is one of the key ingredients of effective management and leadership at every Doll Level.

And the Logical Levels Model is the discipline that forces the right questions to be asked. Once the reader has learnt to live with the fact that the answers they receive to these questions may not be the ones they were expecting, then it's probable that the decisions will be based on facts, not opinions, because the Business Cube is designed to deliver the business facts without the information clutter and PowerPoint hype. Put factual business information through an effective decision-making process with a focussed and driven management team, then you will make the right decisions that deliver your Implementation Plan.

On a personal note, It took about a decade to eventually arrive at a way of working as a BI manager that consistently delivered the results the Client wanted, whatever the circumstances. For some reason, nobody ever showed any interest in the methodology, just the performance results it generated. Which meant I never had to explain, only deliver the Implementation and present those results. Now I've retired, I'm able to share this approach to delivering Business Improvements.

One book, published in 2010, by Bain & Co., entitled *'Decide & Deliver'*, is the closest methodology to the Business Cube and Implementation Model that I've seen in print: it was an inspiration to get me started on this second volume in the Business Improvement trilogy. So well done to the authors, *Blenko, Mankins and Rogers*: any chance of *'Decide & Deliver 2'*?

So read, enjoy, and hopefully implement business improvements in your business.

Acknowledgements

In a working life, there are a few people that you work with and learn from who leave a lasting impression on your thinking. In chronological order, this book is dedicated to Nicholas Wethmar, Store Manager with British Home Stores in 1974, who showed me how to manage a crisis in the aftermath of a bomb explosion. He also said that 'everything you do today should have been done yesterday', a quote that has stuck in my mind for decades. Rick Chandler for tactical management: Jan Metzger for some brilliant technical work with a very difficult Client over many months: Ray Mills for demonstrating the power of systems within any business that needs to improve performance: Martyn Webber for support and guidance over a six year period: and Lai Phan for some excellent business improvements in difficult circumstances.

In a professional life, there may be a few opportunities that offer a chance to develop different skill sets. Working alone on several BIs. meant I had to be creative about how to deliver the Client's requirements: that's when the Business Cube evolved, first as a box, then pyramid, and lastly in a Cube format. And then the Implementation Model developed from the need to use a training and development approach that could be rolled out quickly and effectively by just one manager. First came a multi-level training model, then the Implementation Model. Pleased to say my bosses often stayed away from my assignments and their Clients. Two reasons: my bosses were never sure how to achieve the BI targets themselves, so they delegated to a stand-alone manager who they could blame if the BI failed. And secondly, they never showed any interest in new tools/techniques/models: I guess if you already know everything, there's no need to learn anything more.

And some words for today's BI leaders. There's never been a better time to improve your business, or manage somebody's else's business more effectively and efficiently. And if you believe that 'Brexit' and 'Covid-19' are hampering BI initiatives, or the benefits are less than they were, then think about this:-

*'I make observations, having come from the oil and gas world, that we really have **construction projects in infrastructure that look the same today as they did 40 years ago.** There is a huge opportunity to use modern methods of construction and tools that will bring significant improvements in productivity. **I am not talking about marginal percentages, but 30%, 40% improvement.**... You will have to see that step change in productivity and take hours out of the construction of our projects.'* (Nick Smallwood, CEO of The Infrastructure and Projects Authority, giving evidence to the Transport Committee on major transport infrastructure projects: appraisal and delivery, Wednesday 12 May 2021).

Now construction projects can be business improvement initiatives: so the same thinking can apply in both cases. So I would wish Mr Smallwood the best of luck in the quest to improve performance in public and privately funded infrastructure improvements in the UK: and I acknowledge that this need to improve has prompted the writing of this book. And I hope you're inspired to explore the subject of the Business Improvements in more depth.

About The Author

Nick Jones has 35 years of business consulting experience, specialising in Business Analysis, Implementation Consulting and driving Continuous Improvement: BA (Hons) in Business Studies from Birmingham City University, and a MBA from Middlesex University London.

Prior to consulting, I spent 10 years in line and functional management with British Home Stores plc. and Burgerking (UK) Ltd., working in both Operations and with the Training and Development Teams.

As a Consultant and Project Manager, I worked with dozens of Clients across a broad spectrum of industries on a global basis. Many of these Clients were involved in management buy-outs or buy-ins, or were venture capitalists, or had simply acquired businesses that needed turning-around. This book is based on his experiences during this period, and some of the tools and techniques that were created and used to generate significant improvements in performance and profitability with these Clients.

The 'Business Cube' was developed while working independently on BI assignments: it proved invaluable as a **disciplined approach**, and as a means of ensuring that no details had been missed prior to 'going live' with any Business Improvement.

Website:-

www.nbjbusinesssolutions.com

Contact via:-

M: (+44) 7933 024439

nickcbjones59@gmail.com

Lightning Source UK Ltd.
Milton Keynes UK
UKHW051803090223
416667UK00008B/200